LIQUID EDUCATION

Beer

From hop to the perfect pour

WILL HAWKES

Smith Street Books

Contents

BEER: AN INTRODUCTION

Beer has changed. It's no longer just the go-to alcoholic drink for those seeking refreshment on a hot day, or the social lubricant of choice on a Friday night; no, beer is now taken very seriously indeed. These days, you'll find it on the cover of the *New Yorker* and listed alongside Champagnes and Chablis on high-end restaurant menus around the world.

Has beer got ideas above its station? Not really. The drink is still fundamentally the same – give or take a few new hop varieties and a lot of Bourbon barrels – but the way it is perceived has changed. The truth is that there has always been good beer, particularly in its northern and central European heartlands, but there's far more of it now and it's much easier to get your hands on the good stuff. Raw numbers can only tell you so much, but consider this: the US has gone from less than 90 breweries in 1978 to around 3500 today, while the UK has leapt from 142 in 1980 to 1500. Australia has experienced similar growth. There are even 700 breweries in France, for goodness sake. We all live much closer to a brewery than we used to, and many of them make excellent beer.

Why should anyone beyond hopheads and statisticians care? After all, wine has experienced a similar boom, and cider is not far behind. Here's why: beer is hugely more diverse in terms of flavour, and it boasts an immensely energetic homebrewing culture.

Many of the world's most feted brewers – from Doug Odell of Colorado's Odell Brewing Company to Mikkel Borg Bjergsø of Mikkeller, Denmark's famous gypsy brewery – started at home. Prices may have risen at the bar, but beer's culture remains resolutely democratic.

Not only that, but the energy in beer culture means the drink continues to evolve in a fascinating fashion. New hops arrive on the scene annually, and fresh approaches are a daily occurrence. There's a sense that beer today is like pop music of 30 or more years ago; an outlet for creativity and an increasingly significant part of Western culture. That might make people scoff, but in the city of the Rolling Stones and the Clash, breweries cause as much of a kerfuffle as bands these days. As music venues close, pubs continue to convert to good beer.

There has also been a proliferation of styles. If you went to a pub in Australia 30 years ago, 99 times out of 100 you'd end up drinking pale lager made by an industrial brewer. In the UK, you might have also had the option of cask ale, but there was no guarantee. Now, styles that were barely heard of back then are common in the best pubs in Melbourne and London: Saison, Rauchbier, Altbier, and barrel-aged barley wine.

This new openness is taking beer beyond its traditional heartland. For most of the 20th century, beer was a resolutely down-to-earth drink, associated with the most unpretentious aspects of any society. Aussies took slabs of ice-cold lager down to the MCG to watch the cricket; Englishmen downed pint after pint of weak, cheap Mild (and later, lager) at the pub. That culture still exists, but a new vision of beer has been created alongside it. You can spend upwards of US$50 on a bottle of beer now (whether it'll be worth it depends on what you expect from such a purchase, I expect).

9

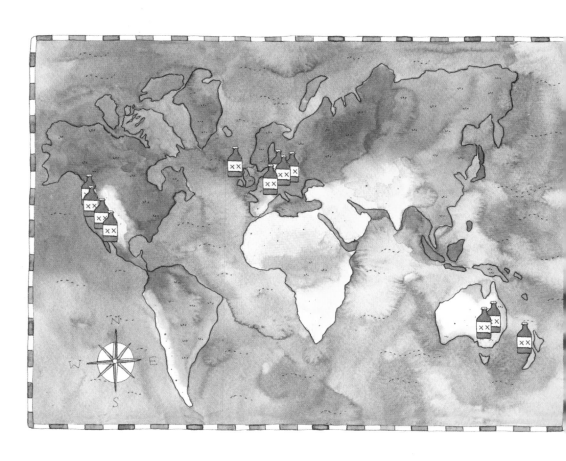

THE CRAFT BEER MOVEMENT
HAS GROWN EXPONENTIALLY
OVER THE LAST 10 YEARS.

This new culture has done much to revive interest in traditional craft brewing, whose heart still beats all over Northern Europe. Places like Brussels and Bamberg, in the centre of Germany, have always been locations of pilgrimage for the committed drinker, but they are even more so today. There are new places to visit, too – from breweries located along the American pacific coast from Seattle to San Diego, to Wellington in New Zealand, and increasingly in Melbourne, too. Beer's heart may be in Europe but its pulse is felt most strongly elsewhere these days.

There are downsides. Prices are up – and not just of good beer, either – and quality is not always what it should be. The rush to jump on the bandwagon means there are some breweries who do not make good enough beer. There will likely be a shakeout at some stage in the next few years, during which some breweries may go to the wall. Drinkers should always favour flavour and quality over novelty.

It's easy to be cynical; the word 'awesome' gets a lot of play in the beer world these days, which is a sure sign that some critical faculties have been thrown out of the window. But then you taste a beer like Two Metre Tall's Cleansing Ale, which, a year after packaging, has a beautiful crystal-clear tartness that refreshes the palate, and you're reminded of what it was that you loved about beer in the first place.

The beer lover has never known such a panoply of flavours or such daily crises of choice. Beer has burst out of its straightjacket and – even if some of the results are gimmicky, such as beer brewed with beard yeast – the results can be stunning. There's never been a better time to enjoy the world's favourite long drink.

A BEERY HISTORY

Any attempt to tell the story of beer is beset with danger. Few subjects are so suffused with misunderstandings and (sometimes deliberate) untruths – from the monk who apparently smuggled lager yeast into Bohemia from Bavaria under his habit (allowing the first golden lager to be brewed), to the origins of porter as a replacement for a kind of beer mixture called 'Three Threads'. If something sounds too good to be true, then it probably is.

The Ancient World

One thing is clear: the story of beer stretches back many centuries.
It has even been claimed that the desire for beer (and its main
constituent part, grain) was what motivated early humans to move
from a hunter-gatherer existence to an agriculture-based society –
an appealing, if unproven, theory.

What we do know is that the Sumerians (who lived in what is modern-
day Iraq between 5000 and 2000 BC) were keen beer drinkers. They
consumed a thick porridge-like brew, which is celebrated in verse:
Inanna and the God of Wisdom, which describes a pair of gods in the
act of drinking beer; and *Hymn to Ninkasi*, a song of praise to the
goddess of beer, which also includes the first written brewing recipe:
"You are the one who waters the malt set on the ground."

Later, the Babylonians and Egyptians were also keen consumers of beer, but not everyone was so intoxicated. Some suggest that the reason wine is still held in higher regard than beer is because the Ancient Greeks – and their cultural offspring, the Romans – took against it. The Roman senator and historian Tacitus wrote in his monograph *Germania* that "...the Teutons have a horrible brew fermented from barley or wheat, a brew which has only a very far removed similarity to wine."

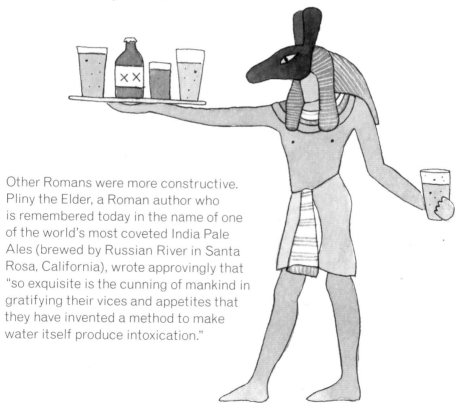

Other Romans were more constructive. Pliny the Elder, a Roman author who is remembered today in the name of one of the world's most coveted India Pale Ales (brewed by Russian River in Santa Rosa, California), wrote approvingly that "so exquisite is the cunning of mankind in gratifying their vices and appetites that they have invented a method to make water itself produce intoxication."

ABBESS HILDEGARD

Middle Ages

Hildegard of Bingen (1098–1179) was an impressive figure. Among other things, this German Abbess was a writer and philosopher who, in 1150, produced an extensive work called *Physica* about the properties of plants and animals. The significance of this tome was that it was the first to record the use of hops to preserve beer – the quality that (for all the excitement over the flavour and aroma you get today) was the key factor in their introduction to brewing. "As a result of its own bitterness it keeps some putrefactions from drinks, to which it may be added, so that they may last so much longer," she wrote.

The use of hops spread around Europe, and by the 15th century hopped beer had landed on English shores. Its arrival represented a challenge to the established order; English ale contained no hops while the interloper, beer (a distinction which no longer exists), was hopped. The latter soon gained a foothold but ale – in its original, un-hopped form – remained popular for many years to come.

But ultimately, the impact of the preservative value of hops could not be understated. Because hops meant beer could be kept for longer, bigger batches could be brewed, meaning bigger breweries could be built. The ascent of hops shifted the nature of brewing; where once it was a kitchen industry, now it gradually became bigger and bigger business.

Industrial Revolution

Modern beer as we know it was born in the heart of London, capital of the world's first industrial nation. It was here that porter – actually a souped-up version of the brown beer then popular in London, named for the street and river porters who carried goods around the city – was first brewed in the early 1700s. Why is that important? Because porter, the forerunner of the dark beers that are today generally known as stout, was the first beer to come out of the Industrial Revolution, and its emergence foreshadowed some huge innovations across central and northern Europe.

By the start of the 19th century, there were a number of huge brewing concerns in London – Barclay Perkins, Whitbread, Truman – all of whom survived well into the 20th century (the latter, has recently been revived in East London). Barclay Perkins was the world's largest brewery for a significant chunk of the 19th century, producing 337,600 barrels in 1815, the year of the Battle of Waterloo, and almost 420,000 in 1851.

Beer was brewed on a huge scale. The size of London's brewing industry can perhaps best be illustrated with reference to the London Beer Flood of 1814, when a huge vat – containing over 600,000 litres of beer – at the Meux Brewery in central London burst, causing other vats to do likewise. A huge wave of beer washed over the neighbourhood, destroying homes and killing eight people.

India Pale Ale

The perspective of history can often overstate matters. Take the emergence of IPA, for example: its place in beer history is distorted with facts often muddled because it's the style that fascinates so many drinkers now. Did it need to be strong to survive the four-month journey from the UK to India? No, and by the standards of the day it wasn't (at 6–6.5% ABV) a particularly punchy beer. Was it invented by a London brewery called Hodgson's at the end of the 18th century? No, he was just the most successful of those brewers who exported this type of pale ale (it wasn't called IPA until later). Pale beers – and pale, of course, is a matter of perception – had been brewed in the UK for many years before Hodgson's came along.

What is clear, though, is that brewers in England's Burton-upon-Trent – such as Bass and Allsopp – took up the cudgel after Hodgson's destroyed their dominance of the trade by foolishly offending the East India Company, the concern that controlled British trade with India. The ascendancy of Burton beer in India reflected the changing balance of power back in the UK: by 1880, Bass was the world's biggest and most famous brewery, leaving the great London names very much in the shade.

Bass, and its Burton rivals, benefitted from at least two crucial factors: the arrival of the railway in this Midlands town in 1839, which opened up new markets in London and beyond; and the famous Burton well water, which is rich in Gypsum, a hydrated form of calcium sulphate, gave their pale beers a big advantage. Gypsum gives a crisp, dry edge to beers brewed with it, which is perfect for pale, hoppy beers like IPAs. Such is the quality of Burton water that brewers all over the world now 'Burtonise' their water by adding calcium sulphate.

Lager

Burton's hoppy ales were not the only great pale beers to emerge in the 19th century; indeed, despite their popularity, they were probably not even the most important. Perhaps the most significant development in 19th-century brewing took place in Pilsen – then part of the Austrian Empire, now a city in the Czech Republic. It was here that Bavarian brewmaster Josef Groll brewed the world's first pale lager, the Pilsner. This beer, named for the city it was born in and the ancestor of all today's golden lagers, is still world-famous as Pilsner Urquell (which, translated from German, means 'Pilsner's Original Source').

Pilsner's iconic beer – now a cherished Czech icon – is actually the creation of pan-European influences. The malting technology that produced its golden colour originated in England, while the yeast came from Bavaria (albeit not concealed by a monk's habit). Golden lager, as we know, went on to conquer first the Czech Republic and then the world.

Pilsner did, however, struggle to gain popularity in Munich, the capital of Bavaria and a city used to regarding itself as the capital of lager, although eventually it succumbed, after a fashion. The most forward-looking brewery in Munich at that time was Spaten, run by two men called Gabriel Sedlmayr, the Elder and Younger. During the 19th century, Spaten was involved in a number of innovations (and a case of industrial espionage, when the younger Sedlmayr, travelled to the UK with Austrian brewer Anton Dreher and came back with a suitcase-full of useful information about yeast, malt and more besides). The most significant of these was the release of the first Helles, Munich's pale, malt-accented answer to Pils, in 1894.

Since then, pale lager has conquered the world to the extent that when most people say beer, they mean Pilsner. The two places it was resisted (with the exception of the Rhineland, where many still prefer the top-fermented Alt and its local rival Kolsch) were Britain and Ireland, at least until the 1960s, 70s and 80s, when it finally surpassed ales for sales.

In recent years, though, this dominance of pale lager – clean, inoffensive, mostly brewed to an immaculate standard without too much concern for character – has helped to sow the seeds for a desire to revive beers with variety and flavour, and to seek out beer styles from the past.

The Arrival of Craft Beer

The term 'craft beer' is liable to cause offence. The literal-minded insist all brewing is industrial; the definition-obsessed splutter that it means nothing; and die-hard microbrewery loyalists make the reasonable point that it has been hijacked by big breweries. No matter. When we talk about what has happened over the past 40 years, it is the best term available; it expresses the passion for flavour, the fervour for creativity and the small-scale nature of what has taken place.

Which is what? Well, craft beer has its roots in two nations: Britain and the United States. In the former, consolidation in the 1950s and early 1960s was followed by the rise of tasteless keg beer in the place of Britain's traditional cask beer; the response was the Campaign for Real Ale, or CAMRA for short, founded in 1971. Despite not really knowing the difference between keg and cask beer at the outset, the founders of CAMRA – four journalists from north-west England – knew the keg didn't taste as good. Their approach struck a chord with the British public, and the campaign went on not only to save cask ale but to become the predominant voice of 'good' beer in the UK, and perhaps the world's most successful consumer campaign. Overall, it has played a huge role in defending good beer in a democratic and often intelligent way.

A little later that decade, a similar feeling of discontent with mass-produced beer was beginning to stir across the Atlantic. Homebrewing gained popularity, particularly after President Carter's administration made it legal in the late 1970s. The equipment and ingredients were basic at best (bags labelled just 'hops' rather than specifying the variety) but these new brewers – who were often inspired by and obsessed with recreating classic British styles – stuck with it.

New breweries began to open on both sides of the Atlantic in the late 1970s and 1980s. New Albion, which – not surprisingly given the name – focused on English-style beer, opened in Northern California and proved very influential. Sierra Nevada followed soon afterwards and, thanks to some great beer, a remarkable commitment to quality and a bit of luck, has survived to this day.

America and Britain began to diverge in the 1990s. Small British breweries, in the main, stuck to classic British styles like bitter and best bitter (with the occasional foray into dark beers like porter), whereas their American counterparts began to experiment with beers from further afield. They started exploring the beers of Belgium and Germany, and creating their own riffs on European classics.

But perhaps even more important than the revival of different beer styles was the emergence of different hops. America has exported hops since at least the 19th century, but things changed in the 1980s with the growing popularity of Cascade, the mainstay of Sierra Nevada Pale Ale. Since then, hop-mania has really kicked off with the arrival of Simcoe, Amarillo, Citra and others. It's these hops – with their citrus, tropical-fruit, piney, dank flavours – that have perhaps spread the gospel of craft beer around the globe more than anything else.

Other countries have joined the fun. In Europe, Italy and Denmark, the craft beer scene has exploded into life, with breweries like Birra Del Borgo, Birrificio Italiano and Mikkeller driving change. Britain, initially conservative, is now home to an at-times riotous creative scene. On the other side of the world, New Zealand boasts a disproportionate number of great breweries like Yeastie Boys and The Garage Project. Australia now has a thriving scene centred around Melbourne, which is home to the annual Good Beer Week, one of the best around. Fantastic beer is being brewed in Brazil, Japan, South Africa... the list goes on.

Everywhere you look, there's a great brew to be had.

HOW BEER IS MADE

The process of brewing is probably better understood now than it has been for a long time. Not by brewers, the cream of whom have always known their stuff, but by the public. Not only is a more diverse variety of beer now available than at any time in living memory, but more and more people are also brewing themselves, using equipment that ranges from not much more than a bucket to some hugely sophisticated kit.

There is huge interest in homebrewing now. Fuelled by an interest in flavour and a desire to experiment, drinkers across the world are making beer at home. This revolution has been led by America, where there are more than a million homebrewers and important breweries have been founded by people who started with a pan and a bucket at home. People like Doug Odell, founder of Sierra Nevada, whose interest in beer was first piqued by a neighbour during his teenage years.

Much has changed since Odell – the man who founded the brewery of the same name, in Colorado in 1989 and one of the craft-beer world's elder statesmen – got started in Southern California in the mid-1970s. At that time, homebrewing was theoretically illegal in the US, and hops and malt were just that – there were no varieties, just bags labelled 'hops'. Now, there are homebrewers who have a more sophisticated set-up than some professional operations. The quality of equipment and ingredients available is superb, and not just in the USA.

Brewing is relatively straightforward, but it does require attention to detail. This chapter is a summary of the brewing process and how it varies in different brewing cultures, but if you're looking to brew at home and therefore need a more in-depth treatment, it's probably best to look elsewhere. A good place to start is John Palmer's *How to Brew*, which is available for free online.

Brewing can be broken down into three key stages: the brew itself, fermentation and finally packaging.

The Brew

Firstly, the grain must be crushed — or 'milled' — in a way that exposes the all-important starch, but leaves the husk largely intact. The starch is crucial for the brewing process, and the husk contains material that would be detrimental to beer quality if it were broken up.

Once the grain has been milled, it's ready for the mash tun. This is where the process of mashing (mixing grain with hot water, often referred to as 'brewing liquor') takes place. The mixture is heated to around 67°C (153°F), which enables two enzymes (Alpha Amylase and Beta Amylase) to convert starch into sugar. Alpha's efforts produce drier, more highly attenuated beers, whereas Beta produces sweeter beers, so the temperature is crucial in terms of how the final beer will taste.

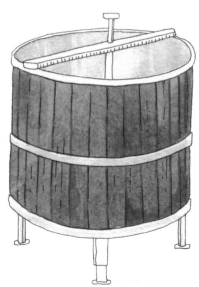

MASH TUN

This process – which extracts colour as well as sugar – produces a porridge-like mixture (wort) and a sensational sweet breakfast cereal aroma. The flavour of the wort reflects this, and it is sometimes known as 'brewers' breakfast'. It's here that the beer's strength is decided; put simply, the more convertible starch there is, the more sugar the yeast will eventually have to convert into alcohol.

Once the brewer is satisfied that the process is complete, the wort is separated from the spent grains (which are often used as animal feed). In traditional British brewing, this takes place in the mash tun, but continental brewing adds another step to the brewing process in the form of a lauter tun, which is essentially a large sieve. Both approaches include sparging, where extra water is added to the grain to ensure that the sugars are fully extracted.

In the English tradition, this second, sparged batch may sometimes be blended with the initial wort in different ratios, thereby producing beers of varying strengths. This process is known as parti-gyling, and it's still used – at Fuller's in London, for example, where Chiswick Bitter, London Pride and ESB are made this way.

Then there's the decoction mash, which is used in the Czech Republic and Germany. This process involves removing a proportion of the mash, boiling it, and returning it to the main mash. Advocates say this ensures that you get a fuller malt character and a deeper golden colour, but critics insist it's no longer necessary given advances in malt and brewing science. Whoever you believe, a number of superb beers are made this way: Pilsner Urquell, for example, is made using a triple-decoction mash.

The wort is then transferred to the kettle (sometimes known as the copper, courtesy of the metal from which they were once made; it's normally stainless steel now), where it will be brought to a rolling boil. This is done for a number of reasons (including sterilisation of the wort and coagulation of proteins, both crucial for the beer's stability), but the key one is to extract bitterness and flavour from the hops, which are added at this stage. The first to go in are bittering hops, chosen for their high-alpha acid, which remain there for 45–90 minutes. The hops used at this stage tend not to be aromatic since most of them will boil away, but they do add bitterness (as the name suggests) and preservative qualities to the beer.

BEER KETTLE

It's later that hops intended to give beer aroma are added. Some may be added 30 minutes before the end of the boil, while others go in during the final minutes or when the heat has been turned off, depending on the desired effect.

Most kettles are now steam-heated, but an older tradition – that of direct fire – still exists, and contributes important flavour and colour to a number of well-loved beers. Most notable, perhaps, is Saison Dupont, the Belgian classic, which owes its golden colour and the sweet element of its flavour to caramelisation that occurs in the kettle courtesy of direct heat.

The wort then enters a whirlpool, where the detritus from brewing – spent hop pellets, coagulated protein, for example – is separated from the liquid, collecting in a central pile due to the spinning motion of the wort. Some breweries use a different method to achieve this same goal using a hopback, a piece of equipment that filters the beer through a layer of whole-leaf hops. A hopback can also be used to add additional hop character to a beer.

Next, the wort must be chilled as quickly as possible in order to prevent off-flavours. This happens in a heat exchange, where the hot wort runs alongside cold water, cooling the wort down and heating the water, which can then be used in brewing. The wort is cooled to 20–22°C (68–72°F) for ales, and 7–14°C (45–57°F) for lagers, enabling the yeast to do its work at lower temperatures.

Another way to cool the wort is to use a cooler, or coolship: a wide, shallow copper pan, which is placed in the attic of a brewery, into which the wort is pumped. Air flows through vents in the roof, cooling the beer, and hops can also be added here. It's not a method that's commonly used anymore due to the risk of infection from airborne wild yeast, but breweries in the Senne Valley – where wild yeast characters are a crucial part of Lambic beer's flavour – and even some in Franconia, Germany's traditional brewing heartland, still use this method. It is also growing in popularity with some smaller brewers, particularly in the USA but also in Australia, where Melbourne's La Sirène brewery has recently installed a coolship in order to capture the wild character of the nearby Darebin Creek.

Fermentation

The wort now enters a fermentation vessel where yeast is added (pitched). Fermentation is the process whereby the sugars from the malt are converted into alcohol, carbon dioxide and heat. The latter result is why fermentation vessels are chilled; fermenting at too high a temperature can result in some pretty unpleasant flavours and affect the health of the yeast (although yeasts work at different temperatures and some produce great beer at higher temperatures).

Modern methods
Many modern breweries now use upright cylindroconical fermenters made from stainless steel, which are cylindrical at the top, with a straight wizard's hat-shaped cone attached to the bottom. They have a number of advantages over other fermenting vessels: it's easy to draw off sediment, they can be used for fermentation and conditioning (vessels that can do this are called universal tanks, or 'unitanks' for short), it's easy to package beer from a conical fermenter, plus they're easy to clean. In addition, because they're closed they can be placed outside the brewery and carbon dioxide given off in the fermentation process can be collected and used later in packaging.

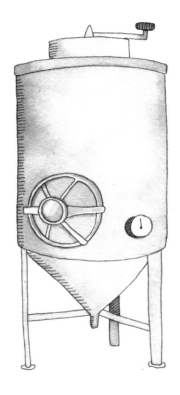

CYLINDROCONICAL
FERMENTER

The Yorkshire Square

There are alternatives to cylindroconical vessels. In Yorkshire, one of the most avowedly traditional counties of England, some breweries still use the Yorkshire Square method. These horizontal conical fermentation tanks were once common, although they fell out of favour partly because conditioning would have to take place elsewhere. The tanks are not always square, but the way they work is always the same: two chambers sit one above the other, with the yeasty head settling in the top layer while the fermenting wort remains below. This makes it easy to draw off most of the yeast.

Some brewers maintain there are other advantages to open fermentation methods like the Yorkshire Square. The yeast lasts longer because it is under less stress, and the beer produced has more ester character than that made in a cylindroconical vessel; that is, fruity flavours – from pear to banana – that are a central component of many traditionally brewed ales. Open fermentation is still regarded as crucial by some of the world's best Weissbier producers, such as Schneider & Sohn in Kelheim, Bavaria. At Staffelberg-Bräu in Franconia, head brewer Karl-Heinz Wehrfritz insists open fermenters are better since they allow the brewer to keep a closer eye on fermentation.

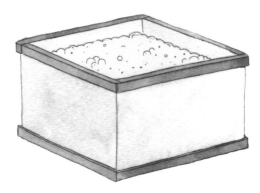

Fermenting in wood

At one time, fermentation in wood would have been the norm. There are obvious sanitation concerns – wood is far harder to keep clean than stainless steel – but it's still cherished by many breweries, such as Marston's in Burton, England. This is the last British brewery to use the Burton Union system, whereby a series of large, linked wooden casks are connected to a communal trough where yeast, expelled from the barrels during fermentation, collects. The wood doesn't actually affect the flavour of the beer at Marston's – they use old casks to avoid this – but it does at Firestone Walker in California, where a version of the Burton Union is used to produce a number of the company's beers.

A number of breweries – from traditional concerns such as Cantillon in Brussels, to Russian River in Santa Rosa, California – use wooden barrels for fermentation. This is done for a number of reasons: wild yeasts can live in wood, which add a unique flavour to beer, while some breweries use barrels that have done service holding whisky or wine. This adds complexity to a beer's flavour: vinous notes from a Chardonnay barrel, for example, can work well with a Saison. There's also the question of how fermentation takes place in a barrel: it's a still-evolving art and it's no surprise that Californian and Australian brewers are leading the way, since the wine revolution in those countries has gifted them some key understandings of how fermentation in barrels progresses.

Ale v. lager

Ale takes less time to fully ferment than lager, as the latter works more slowly in cooler conditions. All things being well, an ale will complete primary fermentation in two to five days, while a lager will take longer, depending on the yeast and temperature. An ale will be conditioned for perhaps a few weeks before it's ready for packaging, whereas lagers can be conditioned for several months.

Secondary fermentation

In the case of British cask ale, secondary fermentation describes the process by which beer completes its fermentation in the cask from which it will be served, sometimes aided by the addition of priming sugar. It's a technique that gives cask ales their soft mouth-feel and gentle carbonation.

Another method, known as krausening, is a German technique where actively fermenting wort is added to the beer in order to re-start fermentation. It's most commonly used to 'finish' beer off, by stimulating carbon dioxide production in a closed tank, thereby conditioning the beer. It's often said that krausening can reduce off-flavours.

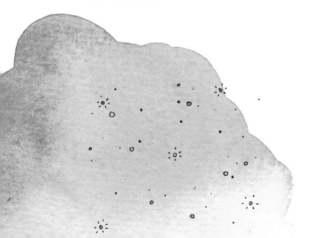

Filtering

Once fermentation is complete, most beer is then filtered to remove any remaining debris, be it yeast or hop particles. Some breweries choose centrifugation, whereby the beer is whirled around at high speed, forcing out denser material, but other brewers don't filter at all, believing (correctly, in my view) that filtering robs beer of flavour, although it can mean that there are small deposits in the bottom of their bottled products, or that the beer pours hazy. Some beer styles – notably Hefeweizen – have always been sold unfiltered and cloudy.

Packaging

Putting beer into containers from which it will be served might not seem like the sexiest topic going, and that's probably because it isn't. If you've ever been on a brewery tour, you'll likely have found the brief view of the bottling line to have been of less interest than the brewing equipment. Nonetheless, it does matter in terms of the quality and flavour of the beer you'll drink, so it's worth knowing a little about.

Kegs and casks

Once beers have been conditioned, they're ready to be packaged, most typically into kegs, cans and bottles. Some beer is also put into casks, which are similar in appearance to kegs (contrary to popular belief, they're generally made of stainless steel, not wood), but with sides that curve out in the middle.

However, if you drink draught beer in a bar anywhere in the world then, most likely, it will be served from a keg. This is normally a straight-sided cylindrical container made of stainless steel, with a spoke that goes from almost the bottom of the keg to an opening in the top, from which the beer is extracted by gas pressure. The beer will generally have been pasteurised and filtered before it leaves the brewery.

A new type of keg is being used by some brewers who either can't afford traditional kegs – which require initial investment in cleaning and filling equipment – or who are dissatisfied with the dispense method that pumps carbon dioxide into their beer. It's called KeyKeg, and it consists of a bag filled with beer inside a hard plastic shell. The beer is dispensed by gas being pumped into the space between the bag and the outer shell, meaning the gas doesn't come into contact with the beer. It can also be used to serve keg-conditioned beer, just like cask ale. At the moment, its main disadvantage is that it remains far less robust than traditional kegs, but we can expect to see this technology advance over the next few years.

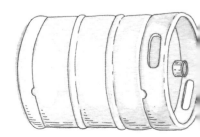

MOST BEER IS SERVED
FROM A STEEL KEG

Cans and bottles

Most, if not all, beer drinkers will have drunk from a can at some stage and then moved on to bottled beer; but there is new excitement gathering, as craft brewers – from Dale's in Colorado to Mountain Goat in Victoria – have begun to use this once-maligned form of container. The advocates – and they are legion – say that cans are much better than bottles for keeping out light, they're more portable and they look great. Critics respond that the difficulty of filling cans means that oxygen pick-up is a problem. Oxygen is finished beer's great enemy (it makes the beer taste stale, among other things), so anything that can reduce its impact is welcomed.

Despite the current sexiness of cans, bottles retain a classier image and when done well, bottling is hard to beat. The best colour glass is brown, as it's the most effective for keeping out harmful light, which can cause a skunking flavour. Bottled-conditioned beer – where a little priming sugar is dropped into each – can also be superb.

Design

It's often said that the key to marketing is to understand that you're selling the sizzle, not the steak. It's a lesson well understood by craft brewers and sometimes (but not that often, despite what critics might say) the packaging is better than the product. The creativity that fuels craft beer goes hand-in-hand with an interest in quality artwork. In London, for example, the artwork of Alec Doherty and Nick Dwyer has been absolutely crucial to the success of Partizan and Beavertown respectively.

The rise of the can has accelerated this phenomenon. Among the first to understand this was San Francisco's 21st Amendment, who have worked with artists including Londoner Joe Wilson to produce not only eye-catching cans but also cardboard six-packs. The latter boasts wraparound artwork that is miles away from traditional beer packaging and the fusty way so much wine is presented.

THE ARTWORK FEATURED ON PARTIZAN BOTTLES HAS BEEN CRITICAL TO ITS SUCCESS

BEER INGREDIENTS: WHAT MAKES BEER GREAT?

For a simple drink, beer can be remarkably complex. It's normally made with grain, hops, yeast and water, which seems straightforward enough but there's huge variety hidden within each of these categories (yes, even water). Not only that, but there are other ingredients added, too – most commonly, fruit and spices.

In this sense, beer is completely different to a one-ingredient drink such as wine, and hops in beer – the sexiest, most lauded ingredient – are not equivalent to grapes. They're the spice, not the soul, of beer. That is not to say that the other ingredients don't play equally important roles – they all contribute to a fine balancing act that results in the many flavours and styles of beer available today.

Grain

A variety of grains – malted and unmalted – can be used to make beer, but the most common is malted barley (malt), so let's focus on that for now. You'll sometimes hear malt described as 'the backbone of beer', and this is basically true. It gives beer its body and flavour, it's the ingredient that makes Pilsner golden and stout dark, and it provides the sugars that yeast converts into alcohol. It's a pretty big deal.

How do you produce malt? Barley undergoes a process of soaking and drying in order to kickstart the growing process. By the end of this stage, each kernel will have tiny rootlets at its base and the moisture content will have risen to around 42%. The process then continues for four to five days in a germination chamber, which comes in a variety of forms, but the most traditional involves a large, tiled floor on which the grain is spread. It is constantly turned in order to keep the grain in good condition. There are still some maltsters that turn the grain by hand, but most are now mechanised.

When the grain is ready to offer up its all-important starch to brewers, the germination process is halted in order to prevent nutrient loss. This is achieved by drying the grain in a kiln or a roasting drum. This step also causes a process known as the Maillard reaction, which produces the bready, nutty, toasty, toffee flavours we associate with malt.

Malt varies in colour depending on the temperature at which it is kilned: a low final temperature of 85°C (185°F) produces a pale malt such as Pilsner malt; a higher temperature of 120°C (248°F) will make a darker malt. For an even darker kernel, the malt is placed in a roaster where it is heated to about 250°C (482°F). The darker the malt, in general, the more toasted, bitter flavours it produces. Brewers can use just a single malt in a beer, or many more, depending on the flavour they're trying to achieve.

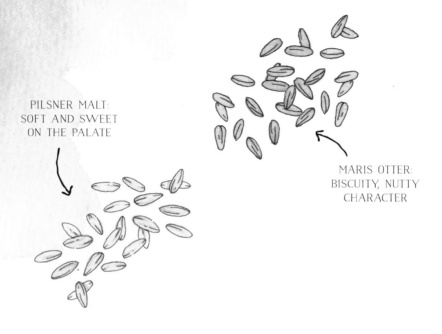

PILSNER MALT:
SOFT AND SWEET
ON THE PALATE

MARIS OTTER:
BISCUITY, NUTTY
CHARACTER

Base malts These are the most important malts, the ones that make up the majority of the malt bill (recipe) for any given beer; other malts are sometimes known as 'specialty malts'. Base malts are generally pale and they provide the enzymes that convert starch into sugar (unlike specialty malts; if a brewer wishes to use only a single malt in his beer, it will have to be a base malt), and plenty of flavour, too. Notable examples include Pilsner Malt, which is exceptionally pale and soft and sweet on the palate, and Maris Otter, a British variety which is prized around the world for its biscuity, nutty character and is often used in session-strength ales.

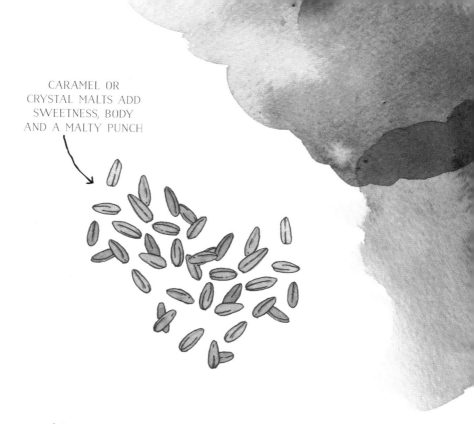

CARAMEL OR
CRYSTAL MALTS ADD
SWEETNESS, BODY
AND A MALTY PUNCH

Caramel/Crystal malts

These are malts that have undergone an extra stewing process during malting, which crystallises the sugars within the kernel. They add sweetness, body and a malty punch to beer. They vary in colour from very pale to dark brown, and cannot be used without the addition of base malts, as they are non-diastatic, meaning they lack the enzymes required to break down starch into all-important fermentable sugars.

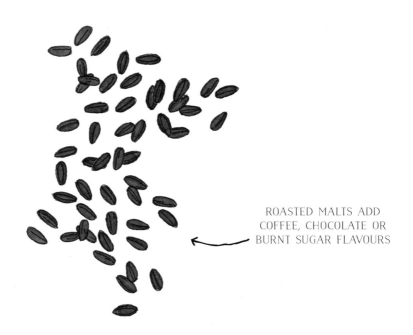

ROASTED MALTS ADD
COFFEE, CHOCOLATE OR
BURNT SUGAR FLAVOURS

Roasted malts and raw grains

The roasting process creates a wide variety of flavours including coffee, chocolate and burnt sugar as well as adding colour to the brew. Darker roasted malts are used in many stouts and porters, where (if used to sufficient quantity) they add an espresso bitterness. It's not just malt that is added to the roaster. Raw grains can be roasted, too, in particular barley. Roasted barley (that is, barley that has not been malted) is a very common ingredient in Irish-style stouts.

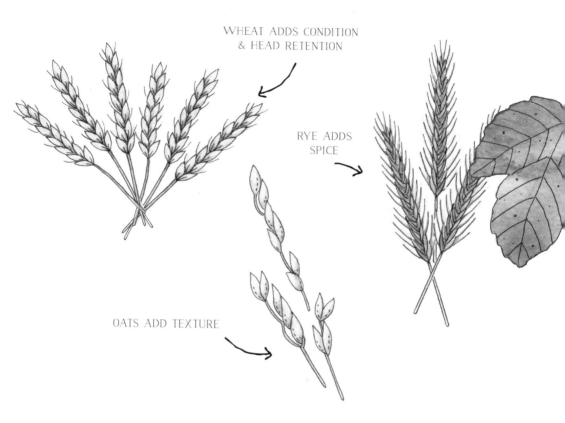

WHEAT ADDS CONDITION
& HEAD RETENTION

RYE ADDS
SPICE

OATS ADD TEXTURE

Other grains and malting ingredients

Wheat is often used, most notably in Bavarian Weissbiers and Belgian witbiers, but also in pale ales to help head retention – wheat malt contains more protein than barley malt, which is reputed to help. Rice and corn are often used in pale lagers, particularly those that are industrially produced, to create a lighter-bodied beer (it certainly isn't to save money: rice is now more expensive than barley malt). Rye and oats add spice and texture respectively.

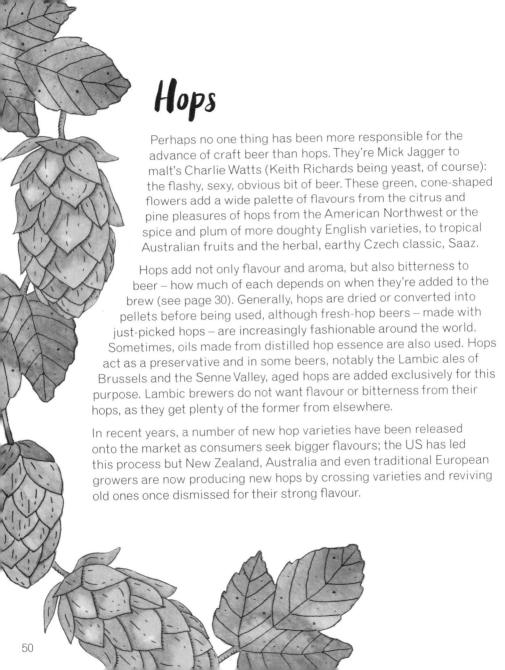

Hops

Perhaps no one thing has been more responsible for the advance of craft beer than hops. They're Mick Jagger to malt's Charlie Watts (Keith Richards being yeast, of course): the flashy, sexy, obvious bit of beer. These green, cone-shaped flowers add a wide palette of flavours from the citrus and pine pleasures of hops from the American Northwest or the spice and plum of more doughty English varieties, to tropical Australian fruits and the herbal, earthy Czech classic, Saaz.

Hops add not only flavour and aroma, but also bitterness to beer – how much of each depends on when they're added to the brew (see page 30). Generally, hops are dried or converted into pellets before being used, although fresh-hop beers – made with just-picked hops – are increasingly fashionable around the world. Sometimes, oils made from distilled hop essence are also used. Hops act as a preservative and in some beers, notably the Lambic ales of Brussels and the Senne Valley, aged hops are added exclusively for this purpose. Lambic brewers do not want flavour or bitterness from their hops, as they get plenty of the former from elsewhere.

In recent years, a number of new hop varieties have been released onto the market as consumers seek bigger flavours; the US has led this process but New Zealand, Australia and even traditional European growers are now producing new hops by crossing varieties and reviving old ones once dismissed for their strong flavour.

Cascade The hop that changed beer. First released onto the market in the early 1970s, Cascade came to prominence throughout the 1980s and 1990s thanks to beers like Sierra Nevada Pale Ale, which uses it to great effect. Today, it's America's most widely grown hop and the most well-known of the C hops (including Citra, Centennial and Chinook among others). It's been planted around the world, in the process demonstrating the impact of environment on hop flavour: the US-grown stuff is potently floral with plenty of tangy citrus, whereas the New Zealand variety is subtler and perhaps a touch peppery.

Citra Each year brings new hops for craft brewers to play with, but few have had a bigger impact than Citra, which has become one of the world's most in-demand hops since its emergence in 2008. As the name suggests, this American hop is powerfully citrus-inclined with plenty of passionfruit and gooseberry character, too. You can find this hop in Oakham's Citra (Peterborough, England) or Feral's Karma Citra (Western Australia).

East Kent Golding English hop-growing has fallen off a cliff over the past 40 years; time-worn, understated classics like Fuggles are not exactly flavour of the month at the moment, and acreage has fallen from nearly 80,000 acres in the late 19th century to under 2,500 today. One traditional hop that does produce some excitement is EKG, a selection of similar varieties that harvest at different times, all grown in East Kent, England, although much of the crop crosses the Atlantic. It can be floral and earthy with gentle plum/soft fruit undertones. The Brooklyn Brewery use lots of East Kent Golding in their East India IPA.

Galaxy

Australia's hop-growing industry has been transformed of late, with the major producer – Hop Products Australia – investing hugely in acreage and variety development. An industry once based on the humble Pride of Ringwood, it now has eccentrically named hops such as Ella and Vic Secret that are in huge demand around the world. One of the most impressive hops to come out of HPA's program is Galaxy, which has proven very popular due to its potent passionfruit character. Seek out Stone & Wood's Pacific Ale if you want to taste Galaxy at its best.

Hallertau Tradition

Germany has more acreage devoted to hop-growing than anywhere else in the world (although the USA is catching up fast and may indeed have overtaken by the time the 2016 harvest is over), and most of that is located in the Hallertau. A number of different hops are grown there, including Hallertau Tradition, bred to replicate the character of the low-yield, disease-susceptible noble variety Hallertau Mittelfrüh. It's subtle, floral and herbal; try Penn Brewery's Pilsner, made in Pittsburgh, or any number of classic German lagers.

Nelson Sauvin

New Zealand doesn't actually grow many hops, but the ones they do produce have proven popular with brewers around the world. The most famous – and most widely grown – is Nelson Sauvin, so named because it is grown in Nelson, at the northern tip of the South Island, and its flavour is somewhat reminiscent of New Zealand-grown Sauvignon Blanc. Its character is clean, gooseberry-inflected and full of vinous astringency. Brewdog's Punk IPA includes plenty of Nelson Sauvin and for locals, Tuatara's single-hopped Sauvinova is a must.

Saaz

Grown in the Czech Republic – notably close to the town of Žatec in Bohemia, after which it is named (Žatec is Saaz in Czech) – this is perhaps the most significant hop of them all. It's the distinctive peppery, soft lemon character in Pilsner Urquell, not to mention a host of other famous pale lagers such as the Czech Budvar. Saaz and other Czech hop varieties are so revered in Žatec that there's a whole museum devoted to them, plus a tiny hop garden right in the centre of town.

Yeast

Not too long ago, yeast's crucial role in making beer was misunderstood; brewers knew that it was essential to brewing but very little about how it worked or even really what it was. Germany's famous beer purity law, the Reinheitsgebot (introduced in Bavaria in 1516 in order to prevent brewers using wheat, which was reserved for bakers) stated that beer must have only three ingredients – water, barley and hops – thereby excluding the addition of yeast. It was not until the 1830s, when German physiologist Theodor Schwann deduced that yeast was alive and caused fermentation, and then the later efforts of Eilhard Mitscherlich and Louis Pasteur, that yeast's crucial, fascinating role in producing beer was fully understood.

All of the yeast strains used to ferment beer come from the species *Saccharomyces cerevisiae*, which converts carbohydrates to carbon dioxide and alcohol, and its close cousin *Saccharomyces pastorianus*, known as the lager yeast (of which, more later). There are a huge number of varieties available, and they each have a crucial part to play in how a beer tastes.

You only have to take a look at the range sold by the big yeast companies, such as White Labs in San Diego, to see what diversity there is. Planning to brew a traditional English ale? WLP002 English Ale Yeast will do the job (as will a number of others). Prefer something with a more Australian character? WLP009 Australian Ale Yeast will help you get the right result.

Traditionally, breweries would maintain a single house yeast, which conveys a certain instantly recognisable character on each of their beers. This is perhaps most noticeable in the UK and Belgium. London's Fuller's Brewery, for example, is famous for the marmalade inflection its yeast gives Fuller's beers, while Harvey's, a brewery based in Sussex, owes its almost cult status to a complex, beguiling character that has much to do with the house yeast.

In Belgium, Brasserie Dupont is famous for its Saison – for many people, the definitive Saison – which derives much of its spicy, earthy, exceptionally dry character from the yeast used. Then, there are the Lambic styles of Brussels and the Senne Valley, whose beers are fermented with wild yeast that blows in on the wind. The subsequent flavour owes a huge amount to this romantic (and increasingly fashionable) method of fermentation.

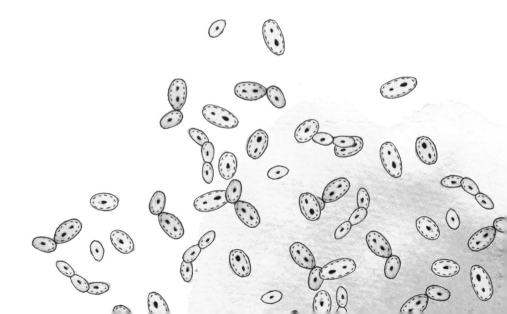

Nowadays, breweries use a wide variety of yeast strains. Goose Island (based in Chicago but with much of its beer brewed elsewhere since it was bought in 2011 by AB InBev) uses more than 15 strains. That's a lot, but it's not uncommon where bigger craft brewers are concerned. If you brew both a traditional English ale and a convincing Bavarian wheat beer, you'll need to use two different varieties.

Yeast plays a central role in the beer world's major schism, which divides ale from lager. While ale yeast is top-fermenting – which means that, in most if not all cases, the yeast rises to the top – lager yeast is bottom-fermenting, meaning the yeast settles to the bottom towards the end of fermentation. The key difference is the temperature at which both do their best work. Ale yeast generally operates between 10–25°C (50–77°F), while lager yeast works between 7–15°C (45–59°F).

This matters because the lower temperature at which bottom-fermenting yeast works is what allows lagers to be brewed. Lager means 'store' in German, and lagers are traditionally slow-fermented in cold storage – a process which results in a more stable product. One of the most famous Czech pale lagers, Budweiser Budvar (which is known as Czechvar in the United States) is kept in tanks for 90 days, although most lager brewers no longer consider this length of conditioning to be necessary.

Water

Water makes up the vast majority of any beer you drink, so it's pretty important, but it's not just significant in terms of volume. It can make a big difference to the flavour of a beer, and the evolution of some beer styles can be attributed to the varieties of water that can be found around of the world. Consider Burton, home of pale ale, and Bohemia, where pale lagers were first brewed. The former boasts hard, calcium sulphate-rich water, which provides the perfect conditions for a hop-forward but balanced ale; many brewers around the world now 'Burtonise' their water in order to replicate this effect.

The water of Pilsen in Bohemia is, by contrast, extremely soft and low in mineral content. The result is a beer where bready malt plays a significant role, balancing out the noble Saaz character for which the best Bohemian pale lagers are rightly renowned.

In fact, water helps to explain why many of the great beer styles emerged where they did. London, where dark beers like porter and stout emerged, has semi-hard water, which contains a high level of bicarbonate that becomes soft when boiled and ensures a high colour extraction from the malt. Dublin, which later became known as the home of stout, has even higher levels of bicarbonate in its water.

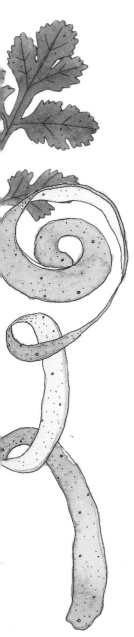

Adjuncts and Flavourings

An adjunct is anything used to replace a proportion of malt in the mash. This includes everything from roasted barley – often used in stout – to peas, which find their way into beers made in Lithuania and Japan. Flavourings, meanwhile, are (as the name suggests) added for flavour. Some ingredients fit into both categories.

Herbs and spices have been used in beer for centuries, especially before the advent of hops. Beers made in the pre-hop era in Europe (often referred to as 'gruit') were made with a variety of herbs and botanical ingredients, or with a single added flavouring. This tradition has been at least partly revived, with modern brewers around the world using ingredients such as heather, ginger, spruce and bog myrtle in their beers. The most well-known example of a flavoured beer in the modern world is Belgium's witbier. Made with a proportion of unmalted wheat, it is traditionally flavoured with coriander and orange peel.

There are a few examples of beers that have survived the hop-focused modern era and still exist in their pre-industrial state. Beers like Finland's Sahti, which is flavoured with juniper, and the farmhouse ales of Lithuania (which boasts a unique and fascinating beer culture that is largely unknown outside its borders) sometimes include a small proportion of peas in place of malt. Then there's Kvass, a Slavic and Baltic drink made with fermented rye bread, that may be flavoured with herbs and fruits.

Rather easier to find are those beers that are flavoured with fruit. The most famous are produced in Belgium, and in the Belgian tradition. Lambic beers steeped with cherries (Kriek) and raspberries (Framboise) are increasingly popular, and traditional versions made by the likes of Cantillon and Drie Fonteinen are much sought-after at the moment. Other fruits, such as peach and blackcurrants, have also been used to flavour Lambic.

Fruit finds its way into beers other than Lambic, too. Breweries around the world are taking advantage of beer's hard-earned new permissive culture to experiment: Ballast Point, for example, add grapefruit to their Sculpin India Pale Ale, while the brewers at Budvar in the Czech Republic have produced a dark lager made with wild cherries.

More unusual ingredients are also being added to beer. Two Birds, based in Melbourne, Australia, produce a beer called Taco. The intention, as the name suggests, is to replicate the flavour of Mexican food, so lime peel and coriander leaf are used. Meanwhile, the New Zealand brewery Yeastie Boys and more recently Marble in Manchester are two of a number of breweries to use Earl Grey tea in a beer.

And finally, a little bit more about adjuncts. It's a word that has negative connotations in the world of beer, where connoisseurs can be sniffy about anything that messes with the 'purity' of their pint. The use of corn and rice by some of the bigger lager breweries in the US (you can probably name them) has given adjuncts a bad name, although they do a fine job of lightening colour and flavour. Sugar has a better reputation, probably because it's used in a number of the best-known Belgian and British ales. Belgians often use a type of sugar called candi sugar, which boosts the ABV without adding body.

Some additions appear to be made for publicity value as much as flavour. In 2013, Rogue in Oregon fermented a beer with yeast from head brewer John Maier's beard. The intention was, so the brewery claimed, to find a 'local' yeast strain to complement local malt, hops and water. The result was Beard Beer, which has garnered media attention around the world. Rogue has also produced a stout made with Sriracha hot sauce, along with a variety of other unusual ingredients.

BEARD BEER - WHERE THE SECRET INGREDIENT IS BEARD YEAST

STYLES OF BEER

The structure of beer styles can make beer seem extremely simple. It's a system that fits every beer into a different group depending on a variety of factors: colour, flavour, aroma, how it's made, its historical roots etc. There's porter and there's pale ale; there's stout and there's pale lager. Easy. Every beer you can imagine fits neatly into one of the boxes and confusion never arises.

Alas, that's not quite how it plays out. As a general guide, styles are handy but the order they bring is illusory. What is the difference between a stout and a porter? How wide do you spread the boundaries of 'pale ale'? (What counts as 'pale' being entirely a matter of perception, of course; in 19th century England, anything paler than a porter counted. Views may be different today).

Many beers don't respect these style boundaries and for someone new to beer, this diversity can be more baffling than enlightening. The American Beer Judge Certification Program – the world's premier register of beer styles, modern and historic, albeit intended primarily to guide homebrewing judges – includes 34 different categories, each of which has a number of styles. IPA, for example, incorporates seven different styles, not including English IPA or Double IPA, which are found elsewhere (it's not clear why). Sometimes it seems all you need to do is add a different hop to a traditional recipe and – voila! – a new style is born.

America's recent awakening to beer is probably at the root of this obsessive categorisation. Style might seem like an American attempt to impose order on the mess of European history. In England, Best Bitter is what the local brewer makes – it might be floral and dry in Kent where the hops grow, and soft and sweet in the West Country, but it's all bitter. Belgians don't obsess over the differences between their many different 'styles' of beer either (or at least they didn't; American influence grows by the year). In Europe, beers cover the whole gamut, spread out fairly evenly between darkest black and palest straw, between incredibly bitter and cloyingly sweet, and so on.

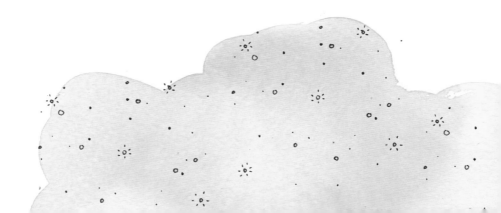

Yet, the popularity of American hops over the past 30 years has brought with it the rise of 'American Pale Ale' and 'American IPA'. You might argue that the rise of Australian hops during the last few years means we can now talk of Australian Pale Ale, too, in the form of Stone & Wood's Pacific Ale, for example. And why not? If we're going to have more than a hundred styles, then the use of Australian hops is the perfect reason to declare a new one.

The concept of beer styles was first mooted by Michael Jackson, without doubt the most influential beer writer of all time, in the late 1970s. Before then, some now well-known beer styles were fairly ill-defined (but no less delicious for that), particularly in Belgium. Of course, people spoke about porter or Pilsner before then, but it was Jackson who set it all in stone and made it such a central part of the beer world.

There are surely more beer styles to come. The next few years promise more innovation (with the one qualification that there is nothing – or at least not much – new under the sun; much of what passes for novelty these days was common practice for Victorian brewers across Europe), which will inevitably result in more styles. And while the idea of style might be unsatisfactory to some, it is likely to be with us for the foreseeable future.

There is one significant difference that is worth knowing even if you don't find the idea of beer styles particularly useful: that between top-fermenting and bottom-fermenting beers. The first – often called ales – tend to have more extravagant flavours; the latter – lagers – are in the main cleaner, having undergone a (sometimes lengthy) conditioning process.

Some Important Beer Styles...

Pale Ale

This style covers a huge variety of beers, from nut-brown, gently satisfying English bitters to straw-pale, hugely bitter and heroically aromatic American Imperial India Pale Ales via Blonde Ales, a fairly vague designation for beers that vary in flavour but are always the same colour. Sometimes, it can seem little more than a catch-all term for any top-fermenting beer that isn't dark.

English Pale Ale

The home of pale ale is Burton in the English Midlands, which became famous in the 19th century thanks to a number of legendary British breweries, foremost among them Bass. At the time, Bass was the world's most famous beer; its unmistakable red triangle (Britain's first trademark) was known across the globe, from France – where its popularity led to supporting roles in paintings by Manet and Picasso – to the United States; the Titanic set out for New York with 12,000 bottles of the famous beer onboard in 1912.

Bitter, as its known in its homeland, has come a long way since then, but it remains a staple on the bar in English pubs. Although only briefly the most popular beer in England – between the demise of Mild in the 1960s and the rise of lager in the 1970s – it is seen as the epitome of English beer. It is a low-ABV (3–4.5%), amber-coloured ale generally served in its home country from a cask rather than a keg, where the beer traditionally undergoes a secondary fermentation, emerging lightly carbonated and hugely easy-drinking. Flavourwise, it varies but you can generally expect a balance of grassy, hedgerow hops and sweet, nutty malts.

American Pale Ale

This form of pale ale first emerged in the early 1980s from Northern California, the crucible of the American craft beer movement. It can seem a little tame these days compared to some of the Double IPAs being brewed around the world, but its influence has been huge. The classic example is Sierra Nevada, which is closely related to its British forebears but nonetheless different: there's little or no yeast character, the malt profile is muted and the hops – as long as you drink the beer when fresh – sing, offering tropical fruit, pine and citrus flavours.

India Pale Ale

The roots of India Pale Ale can be found in London and (subsequently) Burton. It began life as a dry, hop-forward but nonetheless balanced beer that was exported to Britain's colonies (chief among them, of course, India). Recent research suggests that it was shipped flat, but due to the Brettanomyces, a wild yeast that lived in the barrels in which it made the journey, it arrived sparkling and with a character that bears little resemblance to what we think of as IPA today. This fascinating idea demonstrates how our understanding of beer history is still evolving.

The beer enjoyed huge popularity during the 19th century, but its star dimmed, and by the 1980s it was little-known in its homeland (even if there were beers labelled 'IPA' on the market, which were, and are, in the form of Greene King IPA, fairly standard bitters).

It was then that American brewers got their hands on it, gradually transforming the IPA into a very different beast. Nowadays, an IPA is a very heavily hopped, hugely aromatic and often bracingly bitter beer of at least 6% ABV. Then there are Double IPAs, Triple IPAs, Imperial IPAs... One of the most well-known examples, Pliny the Elder (made by Russian River in Northern California) is a great example of the style: 8%, golden–orange in colour, with huge orange peel and mango aromas and flavours; it's remarkably easy-drinking despite a persistent bitterness.

The mania for IPA has seeped deep into the marrow of beer culture. Around the world, but especially in the United States, brewers know that if they put IPA on the label it's more likely to sell. Hence, Belgian IPA, Session IPA, Black IPA, White IPA. If you chuck a few extra hops in, everything can be an IPA.

PLINY THE ELDER –
A GREAT EXAMPLE OF
AN INDIA PALE ALE

Porter/Stout

Porter/Stout What is the difference between porter and stout? Historically, the latter was a stronger version of the former; currently … well, it depends who you trust. Plenty of well-informed beer folk will tell you that the latter is made with roasted barley and the former isn't. Check the recipes of your favourite porters and stouts to see if that distinction stands up to any scrutiny.

Like other classic English styles, porter has enjoyed a renaissance over the past 20 years. It is top-fermented (with the exception of Baltic porter, which is made with bottom-fermenting yeast and cold-conditioned), and is usually very dark brown to black in colour, with flavours of chocolate, espresso, caramel, liquorice, dried fruit and more. It's generally dry, sometimes with an assertive bitterness. Like all historic styles, it has changed a lot since its 18th/19th century heyday, when its flavour profile would have – due to the method of ageing – included tart, even sour notes. Probably the best versions in its native land are Fuller's London Porter and Elland's 1872 Porter; in the US, Anchor's superbly drinkable porter is hard to beat.

But what about stout? Few beer styles are as entirely dominated by one brand as stout is by Guinness – indeed, the name Guinness is probably rather more famous around the world than stout. It's almost identical to porter in look and flavour, although you might find stouts are drier and darker in general (but you might not); they're certainly not stronger. Some stouts, like Guinness, are nitrogenated, which gives the beer a thick, creamy head and less carbonation than other kegged beers.

Guinness is best enjoyed in atmospheric pubs like the Duke of York pub in Belfast, which has a remarkable collection of old Guinness marketing material on the wall, from posters to clocks.

Pale Lager

This is the world's best-loved beer style. It's brewed everywhere, from Kenya to China via St Louis and, of course, Pilsner. The most famous beer brands in the world are all pale lagers, from Budweiser in the USA to Stella Artois in Europe and VB in Australia. In most cases, it's an exceptionally clean-tasting, highly carbonated product, with not a great deal of discernible malt character (it's often made with other fermentable substances, such as rice) and a touch of prickly hops. Served very cold, it's easy-drinking and inoffensive; in other words, it's beer's answer to fluffy white bread and cheese slices.

Not all pale lager falls into this category, though. Pale lager originated in the Czech city of Pilsen, where it was first brewed in 1842, and there's still nowhere better to drink this iconic style. There, you will find Pilsner Urquell served as Nefiltrovany Lezak, unfiltered and unpasteurised. The result is a soft, hazy golden mix of spicy bitterness, caramel and biscuit.

After its popularity took hold, Pilsner's fame quickly spread outwards to Prague and across Europe. Immigrants from central Europe took the style across the Atlantic to the USA, creating not only Budweiser but a host of other big lager brands. The city of Milwaukee, in Wisconsin, to which German immigrants flocked in the 19th century, earned the moniker 'World Capital of Beer' on the back of a number of lager brands, from Miller to Schmidt to Pabst.

The reasons for Pilsner's success are not clear but we can assume that the exodus from central Europe helped, as did serving temperature: very cold lager would have inevitably been popular in a Mid-western summer, or in Australia, or India…

SERVED COLD, PILSNER
IS AN EASY-DRINKING BEER

Alas, most mass-produced pale lagers today don't offer much beyond frosty refreshment, but there are some crackers away from the mainstream. Pale lagers can be roughly divided into four groups: Czech-style (Pilsner), German Helles, German Pils and modern Pils, of which perhaps New Zealand-style Pils deserves particular mention. There are others – including, for example, Dortmunder – but these are the most significant for the modern drinker.

Pilsner

This group includes PU, Budvar, Bernard and other lesser-known versions brewed by the likes of Kout na Šumavě and Únětický. It is made with Bohemian hops – normally Saaz – and Moravian barley. The result can be round, caramel-rich and soft, like Pilsner Urquell, balanced like Budvar or assertively bitter like some of the lesser-known versions. It tends to be a deeper golden colour than German Pils. It's best drunk in its native land, where an acute understanding of how beer should be kept and served heightens the experience.

To the Czechs, the term Pilsner only refers to Pilsner Urquell; other pale lagers are called světlý ležák and they inspired many of the world's most famous brands: at the Hop Museum in Žatec, which lies at the heart of the Czech Republic's most significant hop-growing region, there's an old advert for American Budweiser boasting that it is made with Saaz hops grown in the region (Žatec is the Czech word for Saaz, which is German). Perhaps, before Prohibition, Budweiser once tasted more like the Pilsners of the Czech Republic.

Helles

Over in Bavaria, the breweries of Munich were slow to respond to the Bohemian upstart's growing popularity, but the arrival of German Helles, first brewed by Spaten in Munich in the late 19th century, changed that. Helles is a malt-forward rather than hoppy beer, biscuity and remarkably clean (and hence, drinkable). Munich's finest version is made by Augustiner Braü and further afield, Tegernsee has many knowledgeable fans.

German Pils

This is a more hop-focused beast than its cousin, Helles, and with less malt body than Czech Pilsners. It's bitter – or at least it should be – and full of lemony, grassy notes. It's a clean, refreshing mouthful of beer, with North German examples such as Jever traditionally more robustly hopped. It can still be delightful elsewhere, such as in Bamberg, Germany's greatest beer town, where Keesmann's Bamberger Herren Pils is a crisp delight. Firestone Walker's Pivo Hoppy Pils – brewed with German hops – is an excellent version made on the other side of the Atlantic, while Tipopils (made by Birrificio Italiano) may be brewed in Italy but it's up there with the best that are made in Germany.

Inevitably enough, plenty of Pilsners are now made with New-World hops. It's arguably hops from New Zealand, though, that are best-suited to the job: a beer like Tuatara's Bohemian Pilsner – which is dry, bitter and grassy on the finish – is hard to resist.

Other Lagers

Not all lagers are pale – indeed, at one point in history (a fairly long time ago, admittedly), none of them were. But for much of the 20th century – particularly outside of Germany – that's the only type that got a look in, which is a shame because darker-coloured lagers can be delicious.

Amber lager

As with ale, there's a huge diversity of colours and flavours available to lager lovers. One of the most popular of the darker lagers is Vienna Lager, an amber–reddish Austrian style that has its roots in a fact-finding trip that brewers Anton Dreher and Gabriel Sedlmayr took to Britain in 1833 to learn about new, indirect-fired malt-kilning techniques, which allowed for a more reliable production of pale malt. A few years after they returned to their homelands, they both produced pale-ish beers: Sedlmayr with Märzen (which is, rather confusingly, now sometimes straw-pale as well as amber), and Dreher with Vienna.

Vienna can be a really delicious beer. There's an almost toffee-like sweetness, which balances out an austere, classically central European bitterness; there's toastiness too. This style is popular in Mexico – where it arrived with the short-lived Maximillian I, an Austrian aristocrat who seized the throne for a brief period in the 1860s – and in the USA, where Boston Lager and Brooklyn Lager both fall (just about in the case of the latter, which is dry-hopped in the British style) into this category.

Dark lager

There are many dark lagers created both in Germany and the Czech Republic, where non-pale lagers are enjoying a revival. Dunkel (a close relation of the Czech Černé Pivo) is the most significant, having been the most popular beer in Bavaria before pale lagers pitched up (it remains popular, particularly in Upper Franconia). It's an easy-drinking beer, showing off the toasty, bready characteristics of German malts at their best; there's not a great deal of bitterness and the flavour is clean, without spice or fruit. It's still easy to get your hands on a good Dunkel in Bavaria but rather harder elsewhere, although some good examples exist in the USA.

And then there's Schwarzbiers which are, as the name suggests, black, but the flavour is relatively mild without a great deal of bitterness.

Strong lager

Doppelbock is a bit more complex. This category-defining lager is brewed by one of Munich's big six, Paulaner, in the form of Salvator. It's a rich, sweet, strong, brown beer (7.9% ABV), with an only-just perceptible prickly bitterness on the finish. The best time to drink it is in Munich during Lent, at Starkbierzeit ('Strong beer time'), a kind of mini-Oktoberfest. The televised tapping of the first barrel at Nockherberg – Paulaner's beer hall and garden on a hill overlooking the city – marks the start of two weeks celebrating the end of winter.

RAUCHBIER HAS A
SMOKY FLAVOUR

Rauchbier

One of the most interesting of all lagers is also among the most opinion-dividing. Rauchbier (smoked beer) is produced by two of the legendary brewpubs of Bamberg: Schlenkerla and Spezial. The former is more famous as it is exported all over the world, but for those who enjoy a subtler treat the latter might be a better choice. Subtlety is welcome here. These beers are brewed with malts that have been dried over an open flame, thereby imparting a smoky flavour to the beer, which drinkers have compared to bacon. It's the way most malt would have been dried before the rise of indirect-fired malt kilning. It's an acquired taste, but one worth acquiring; a number of breweries around the world now make beers with smoked malts.

Saison/Belgian Pale Ale

Strictly, speaking, Saison is a pale ale – but it has enjoyed such a surge of popularity of late that it surely deserves to be considered on its own. Its roots are in Wallonia, the French-speaking part of Belgium, where it was (or so the story goes) once brewed to refresh farmworkers during the annual harvest ('Saison' is the French word for season).

Like so many of the world's great beer styles, it very nearly died out. Brasserie Dupont, whose version is the archetypal Saison, were brewing it only very occasionally by the late 1980s. Today, this bone-dry, assertively bitter, spicy, caramel-rich cloudy pale ale is regarded by some of the world's most renowned beer judges (including Brooklyn Brewmaster Garrett Oliver) as among the world's finest beers.

The interesting thing about Saison is how it exposes the weakness of the idea of beer styles. Dupont is the most famous, but there are other saisons brewed in Belgium that are darker, sweeter, and far simpler. Should they form their own style? The answer is probably that it doesn't matter. It has taken off around the world, particularly in the USA, where brewers use it as the perfect backdrop to experiment with hops, wild yeasts, fruit, and other bits and bobs.

Saison is not the only Belgian pale. There are many others, some of which are fairly sweet and uninteresting, but one that deserves attention is Duvel, an 8.8% strong golden ale. It derives much of its character from the yeast, not unusual in Belgium but this particular yeast originates in Scotland, at McEwan's of Edinburgh. It has a herbal, almost boiled candy-like aroma, a lightness that derives from the use of sugar syrup in the mash, and a mouth-coating spice-and-sweet flavour that is extremely difficult to beat.

DUVEL HAS A HERBAL, ALMOST
BOILED CANDY-LIKE AROMA

It also boasts one of the most impressive heads you'll see, courtesy of secondary fermentation in the bottle and a short period of conditioning. Duvel Moortgat, the company that produces Duvel (and that has recently invested in breweries around the world, including California's Firestone Walker), has begun producing annual single-hopped versions of Duvel, which are well worth seeking out.

If Saison is the fashionable face of Belgian Pale Ale, then Orval – that most unique of Trappist beers – represents the heritage. Dry and bitter when young, it's unique yeast (which includes Brettanomyces, or wild yeast) changes the beer over time, adding rustic complexity. Afficionados argue over when best to drink it – it's best to buy six and sample its development for yourself (It's six months, by the way).

Bière De Garde
Across the border in France you'll find Bière De Garde, a close cousin of Saison that has its roots in farmhouse brewing. The flavour is suitably rustic although it is (generally speaking) much sweeter and more malt-driven than Saison. Jenlain – a well-known brand in France – is the market leader, having done much of the heavy lifting when this beer style looked on the brink of extinction during the 1950s and 1960s. It's now undergoing a quiet renaissance in the Nord-Pas-de-Calais region, and elsewhere, even outside of France.

Wheat Beers

Few beers offer the sense of theatre that you get from a properly served Bavarian Hefeweissbier. In its tall, wide-lipped glass with white bubblebath foam billowing up and over the top, it's all rather inviting, and it is undoubtedly in this photogenic form that most beer lovers know wheat beer. But it's far from the only wheat beer.

There are two main beer styles that fit into this category: Weiss beers from Bavaria – such as the aforementioned Hefeweissbier – and witbiers from Belgium. Bavarian wheat beers can be cloudy, golden or dark, and they can be filtered too, which renders them as transparent as the brightest pale ale. The unifying flavour comes not from the wheat – which adds texture and head retention – but the yeast, which offers flavours of banana, bubblegum and clove. Given that, it's no surprise that this is a beer style that people tend to love or hate. Those in the former camp should seek out Schneider Weisse, whose Tap 1 is best enjoyed with white sausage and lederhosened table companions at the magnificent Weisses Brauhaus in Munich.

Belgian witbiers are quite different. Here, it is additional ingredients, such as coriander seeds and orange peel, that drive the flavour, although there's often a touch of acidity, too. Unlike their Bavarian cousins, these wheat beers are made with a proportion of unmalted wheat, an addition revived in the 1960s by a Belgian man called Pierre Celis, who created Hoegaarden. Despite being delicious, Witbier has struggled to catch on among the crafterati, perhaps because Blue Moon, a faux-craft Witbier produced by Molson Coors, is hugely popular in the USA.

There are other beers that use a proportion of wheat yet are not called wheat beers. Wheat is sometimes used in pale ales for texture and head retention; and Lambic is made with unmalted wheat, which can constitute as much as 40% of the mash.

Sour Beers

First things first: to only call these beers 'sour' is an understatement. Yes, there is sourness, at varying levels of intensity, but there's so much else, too. There's rustic complexity (as you'd get in a superb unpasteurised cheese), there's dryness (as in a vintage Champagne), there's lightness and vivacity. Drinking a great Gueuze is one of the beer world's finest experiences.

Gueuze is the offspring of Lambic, which is produced in the Belgian capital, Brussels, and the nearby Senne Valley. Lambic is a type of beer that is fermented with wild yeasts. In the case of Cantillon, a brewery based in the Anderlecht district of Brussels, this occurs when slats in the brewery roof are left open overnight and the breeze blows across the cooling wort, which sits in a coolship – an open, shallow copper pan. The wort is then transferred to wooden casks where a complex, multi-stage fermentation takes place over a period of months and years.

Gueuze is made from a mixture of young and old Lambic (one- and three-years, in the case of Cantillon). This mixture produces a further fermentation in the bottle (the young Lambic still has plenty of sugar in it), which makes the beer sparkling. There are two other traditional Lambic-based beers: Kriek, made with cherries, and Framboise, made with raspberries. At their best, both are delicious.

Lambic has inspired brewers around the world. You'll often hear people say that sour beer is 'the next big thing' which, while overly optimistic (some of these flavours are fairly challenging), is probably true for brewers. In an industry where so much is very closely controlled, the magic (and that's what Jean Van Roy, owner and head brewer at Cantillon, calls it) of Lambic fermentation is irresistible. This is beer's next frontier, a chance for the talented and the not-so-talented to experiment with some fascinating flavours and techniques.

It's no wonder that sour beers have become very fashionable in the United States. Led by the likes of Russian River (Northern California) and Jolly Pumpkin (Michigan), America now produces a huge variety of sour – or wild, if you prefer – beers. Some of them are truly excellent, although – to generalise wildly – you might find they lack the complexity of their Belgian forebears. Like the beer itself, learning to make great Lambic takes time.

There are other beers that fit into this category. Take Flemish Red ales, for example, of which Rodenbach is perhaps the most notable. After a fairly conventional brewing and conditioning process, the beer is transferred to huge oak vats, or 'foeders', where it is kept for as long as two years. It's here that it develops its unique flavour, courtesy of microorganisms that live in the foeders (some of which are more than a century old). The resulting beer is blended with un-aged Rodenbach to produce Classic and Grand Cru; with the latter having more aged beer in the blend. Grand Cru is acidic but also full of fruit characters: cherries, apple, some balsamic vinegar.

Finally, there's Berliner Weisse, a type of beer that has enjoyed a surge in popularity of late, probably because it provides an acidic kick but is much easier (and quicker!) to brew than Lambic. These are wheat beers, made tart by adding *Lactobacillus* to the wort or (less often) by a secondary fermentation in the bottle. Historically, the beer would have included Brettanomyces (wild yeast), too, although this isn't generally the case now.

Dubbel and Tripel

Trappist beers are not in themselves a style, but Dubbel and Tripel – the two most well-known Trappist beers, named for their strength – are. And, while the Trappist badge has proven to be a tremendous marketing ploy, some Abbey beers are often just as good or better than their Trappist cousins.

A Trappist brewery is one that is located within the walls of a Trappist monastery (the place where Trappist monks live), where brewing is undertaken or – and this is key – 'supervised' by monks and where the beer is at least partially fermented. Monks don't actually do a great deal of brewing, except at Westvleteren, where the monks are still actively involved in the process. There are only 11 breweries in the world that may carry the Trappist label, six of them in Belgium. Despite the widespread belief that these beers have been handed down through the ages, the oldest of them – made by Orval and Westmalle – date only from the early 20th century, although Trappist brewing dates back much further.

Dubbel is a brown beer (although it has been known to be blonde – this is another style which bulges and leaks at the seams). The use of candi sugar makes it fairly strong (6–8.5% ABV), yet light and drinkable, with plenty of dried fruit character. There's also spice and clove from the yeast. The finished brew is a daintily balanced beer that has the capacity to surprise.

Its bigger, brighter cousin, Tripel, also derives some lightness from sugar. It's golden, between 8–10% ABV and, at its best, fairly dry with hints of spice and banana. The most famous version is probably that made by Trappist brewery Westmalle, although there are plenty of excellent secular versions, including that brewed by St Bernardus. Indeed, St Bernardus might be the best place to start if you want to try any 'Trappist-style' beers, despite no longer being Trappist, after regulations changed in 1992 stating that Trappist beers could only be brewed within monastery walls. Westvleteren is today regarded as perhaps the finest of the Trappist breweries, if only because its beers are so hard to get your hands on. Generally only available at the abbey where they're made 'St Sixtus', they're revered the world over – the Abt 12 is picked out for particular reverence. It's good, but not that good.

Hybrids

As you may have noticed, styles aren't watertight. But nothing gets the committed style-man more in a tizz than beers that are, strictly speaking, neither ale nor lager. Beers such as Cologne's Kölsch or Dusseldorf's Altbier, for example, which are top-fermented like ales but then lagered like lagers.

The first – Kölsch – is the pride and joy of Cologne. Wherever you go in the Rhine city, you'll find little cylindrical glasses of Kölsch (which means 'of Cologne'; it's also the name of the local dialect) being drunk. It's a straw-pale, gently bitter beer, without a huge amount of depth or complexity, the best being made by Päffgen. It's for drinkers, and Cologne likes it that way; a beer can only be called Kölsch if it's brewed within the city limits, as the category is geographically protected under EU law (brewers outside Europe sometimes flout this convention, probably in the belief that Cologne's brewers have more important things to do than worry about a boutique beer in Melbourne). You sometimes get the impression that Kölsch is an ancient beer, but the first Kölsch was brewed in 1918 and it took until the 1960s for it to become popular in its hometown.

It's really popular now, though, to the extent that Altbier – the favoured drop of nearby Düsseldorf – is hard to find there. Not that wealthy Düsseldorf really minds. And why would they? Altbier (meaning 'old beer') can be really delicious; it's dark-brown, toffee-sweet and resolutely bitter in a way few Kölschs are. The best versions can be found in the brewpubs of the old town: seek out Füchschen and

Uerige. Alt has declined in popularity in Germany over the past few decades but there are versions brewed elsewhere – mainly in the USA but also in Australia (Young Henry's Natty's Alter Ego, for example) and the UK, where breweries like Mondo and Orbit brew their own versions.

COLOGNE.
HOME OF KÖLSCH

BEER AND FOOD

In Brooklyn, New York, there is a restaurant with a Michelin Star. Nothing particularly unusual about that, you might think, except for one thing: this restaurant, Luksus, serves only beer with food. There's no wine – no California Cabernet Sauvignon, no Burgundy, no Champagne, nothing. This makes Luksus unique, since it is the first restaurant anywhere in the world that doesn't have a wine list to win a Michelin Star.

It surely won't be the last; the idea of food and beer has built up impressive momentum over the past decade. You only have to visit Melbourne during Good Beer Week, when most of the city's best restaurants (and there are lots of good restaurants in Melbourne, believe me) host events pairing beer with their food. Even in Paris, citadel of wine, there is now a restaurant (La Fine Mousse) that focuses entirely on the combination of beer and food.

Why this sudden interest? Beer's recent renaissance has followed that of cheese, coffee and bread. A lot of this new interest comes from people who love and understand food, and putting them together seems inevitable. No doubt, too, that breweries and industry groups who have pushed the idea of beer and food as the traditional venue for drinking – pubs and bars – have gone into decline.

But this just describes a fad; what has kept the pot boiling, so to speak, is the fact that in some cases beer is a tremendous partner to great food. Beer has a huge diversity of flavours which means it can match pretty much anything – even if, in my opinion, wine remains the better choice in some cases (it would be pretty daft, for example, to drink anything but red Burgundy with Boeuf Bourguignon).

It's easy to forget, too, that beer has had a long history with food. In Germany and the Czech Republic, traditional meals – hunks of pork, dumplings, sauerkraut and more besides – have always been accompanied by local beer, both pale and dark. In Belgium, food is made with and drunk with beer. There's a restaurant called Les Brigittines in Brussels where you can try Zenne Pot, a traditional Brussels dish made with cabbage, sausage and whelks, and cooked in Cantillon's Gueuze – best served, of course, with a glass of the same beer. It's absolutely delicious.

When does beer work best? Below are some suggestions or starting points. If you're particularly interested in beer and food, you could do worse than to get a copy of Garrett Oliver's *The Brewmaster's Table*, written in 2003 but still the best book available on the subject, or seek out the work of Melissa Cole and Mark Dredge, both of whom have excellent palates and an appreciation for the better things in life.

It's also increasingly common to see beer used in the preparation of food as well as to partner it. Traditional dishes like Carbonnade – a Belgian stew made with beef, beer and a touch of sugar – and beef and ale pie have been joined by a host of more modern efforts, including beer-can chicken, which – and there's no delicate way of putting this – requires you to stick a half-full beer can in a chicken's anal cavity before roasting. The results are apparently delicious, although removing a red-hot can from a chicken's bum before you can eat it is presumably less pleasurable. Beer can also provide an excellent base for a marinade or batter – beer-battered fish and chips, for example, are increasingly popular in the UK.

Cooking with beer will not necessarily give the same results as cooking with wine: it's problematic when deglazing, since a hot pan will cause everything except the bitterness to quickly boil off, and a bitter sauce is not nice. But, beers with significant acidity – such as Gueuze – can do all the things that wine does, while there are many beers that work just as well as wine in slow-cooked dishes.

One note of caution: stronger beers tend to make better partners for food, in my experience. A classic 4% English bitter is wonderful when drunk with friends in the pub but it doesn't always do justice to a plate of food.

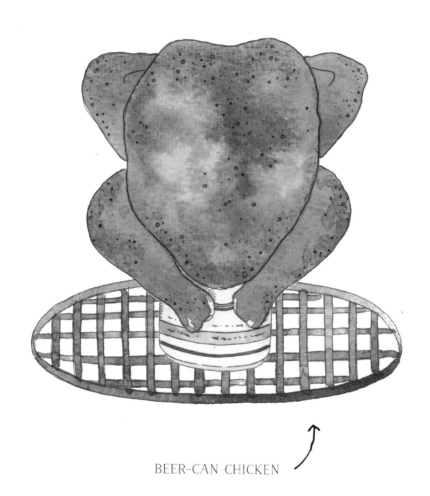

BEER-CAN CHICKEN

Cheese

Any discussion of beer and food must start with cheese. There is no combination more perfectly matched; forget about the fling between wine and cheese, this is the real thing.

Goat's cheese

If you had to choose one beer to have with cheese, it would be Saison – and preferably the classic, Saison Dupont. There's a spicy, lactic character in Dupont that works beautifully with soft and hard goat's cheeses. It is, quite possibly, the ultimate cheese beer.

Blue cheese

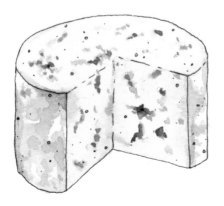

Try a barley wine with an intense blue cheese such as Stilton or Roquefort; the rich, dark–fruit sweetness of the barley wine is the perfect counterpart to the salty, farmhouse tang of the cheese. It sounds like a clash, but it couldn't be more complementary. Big full-bodied stouts, with their roasted richness and some sweetness, also work well. To be honest, there aren't many beers that don't go well with a great blue cheese.

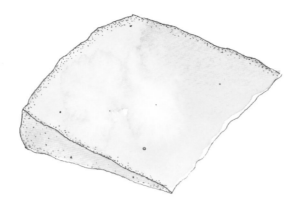

Cheddar

A great cheddar such as Montgomery's, which is made in Somerset (the home of this great cheese), is deep, rich and nutty, with a sharp tang. An IPA – both classic English and modern American iterations – work well here, but my preference is for the former. Its bitterness works well with the cheddar's sharpness and there's a supporting richness and sweetness that grabs onto the fattiness of the cheese.

Best of the rest: from gruyère to camembert

Alpine cheeses, such as gruyère, Beaufort or raclette, are fantastic with beers that have a deep, complex brown-sugar sweetness, such as doppelbocks. Washed-rind cheeses, with their wild, farmyard tendencies, are a natural partner for yeasty Lambic-style beers such as Gueuze. Earthy, mushroom-and-cabbage-inclined soft cheeses like Camembert work a treat with something bold and balanced like Altbier.

Meat

Beef

Few culinary matches are as much loved as steak and red wine. It is sophistication on a manageable scale, an unpretentious taste of French culture but, you know, still steak. It might seem like there's no great point in suggesting an alternative, but there is one: toasty, malty brown ales (if you can drag yourself away from dreams of checked tablecloths and snooty waiters). The main reason for this is a chemical process called the Maillard Reaction (named after Frenchman Louis-Camille Maillard, but let's forget that for now). It's the transformation that takes place when you sear or grill a steak: the browning, the caramelisation, the flavour. But this reaction doesn't only occur with steak; it also happens with bread, coffee, fries – and malted barley, too. This means that there's a natural partner for steak in beer, with brown ales, porter and other darker-hued beers being the most suitable.

Roast beef also goes through a chemical process and, given its significance in the UK, a British-style beer such as Fuller's ESB or a porter pairs with it nicely. There's a balance of flavours in the classic combination of roast beef with potatoes, vegetables and gravy – salt, fat, some sweetness – that works wonderfully with the malt base of strong bitters while allowing hoppy top notes to sing.

Beer is equally handy when it comes to stews, and in Belgium and the UK such dishes are frequently made with beer. There tends to be a richness to these dishes that requires something a little more hefty, which is where Dubbel – with its strength, spice and mouth-coating complexity – comes in.

For barbecued food, and by barbecue I mean the ultra slow-cooked, smoke-enhanced dishes from the southern states of the USA, smoked malt beers are a natural partner. At Southpaw, a barbecue restaurant in San Francisco with a small brewery attached, you'll find a remarkable selection of smoked foods (meat and otherwise) matched to beers that derive their character from smoked malt, or smoked ginger, or smoked hops – anything goes, it appears, as long as it goes with the food. Replicating your own smokehouse and microbrewery might be a bit complicated at home, but there are plenty of beers available made with smoked malt – first among them Schlenkerla Marzen, a smoked amber lager from Bamberg in Germany. Alaskan's smoked porter is another good option.

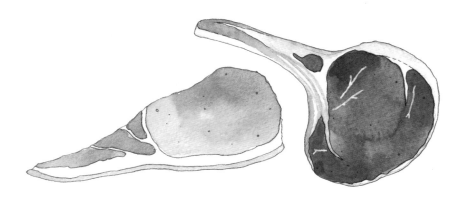

Pork A naturally fatty meat, pork is an obvious partner to beer, something that becomes clear when you look at the cuisine of Germany, and Bavaria, in particular. At Kachelofen in Bamberg, the menu takes in not only bratwurst and pork knuckle but also shoulder – cooked low and slow with beer – and Kesselfleisch, a dish that incorporates more parts of the pig than you knew existed. The beer served here is either smoked dark lager or crisp light–amber pils: perfect matches for the heft and fat of the food.

Pork sausages also pair wonderfully with beer; however, there are so many varieties that a generic match isn't that useful, although an amber lager, like Boston Lager, or an English-style IPA (with more malt–hop balance than the American versions) will happily match myriad sausage flavours. Something with garlic and thyme, like a Toulouse sausage, works beautifully with the bone-dry spice of a Saison, while smoked German sausages cry out for smoked beers.

The same is true of ham and gammon when they're smoked – and when they're not, try a witbier, with its peppery, citrus-laden flavours and mouth-coating richness.

Roast pork calls for something a little cleaner, like a Dunkel.

Lamb In my view, lamb (plus hogget and mutton) is the best meat of all. A leg or shoulder, well-covered with fat and roasted with rosemary and garlic, is hard to beat, but you'll need a beer with particular qualities to match it. Something with decent bitterness and a hint of sweetness, such as Altbier, a Dubbel or an American brown ale works well.

Lamb chops, which can seem old-fashioned but are nonetheless delicious, work well with both a Dunkel (a Bavarian lager with plenty of melanoidin character to match the charred meat) and an American pale ale, whose hops cut through the fattiness. A number of Northern European stews – most notably Irish Stew and Lancashire Hot Pot – work perfectly with roasty stouts like Guinness Original.

Fish In Northern Europe, there is a long tradition of smoked and preserved fish, so it's no surprise that dishes such as smoked haddock or pickled herring find a happy partner in the world of hops and malt. Smoked fish, in all its permutations, works wonderfully with crisp, hoppy Pilsners, or beers made with smoked malt. Pickled fish, meanwhile, almost demands a hoppy, herbal Pils of the north German tradition.

Less powerfully flavoured fish also works with beer. The tropical hop-high notes in an American-style pale ale are great with crab, while Witbier, with its acidity and spice, is another versatile match for any number of different seafood dishes, from mussels to fish cakes.

Chicken

This is often used as a blank slate, a solid piece of cheap-to-produce animal protein to which other, bolder, often spicy flavours are added. In its best form, though, it can be as delicious and satisfying as any meal. Like red wine and steak, it's hard to go wrong with beer and roast chicken. Take a chicken and roast it with thyme and rosemary, for example. Such simplicity responds well to beers that are balanced, with a certain amount of residual sweetness: a Bière de Garde, perhaps, or a traditional dark bock, but a brown ale will also do the job quite nicely.

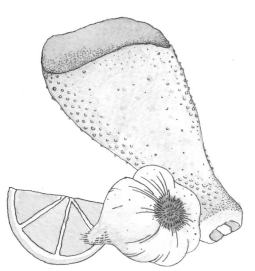

Add lemon to a chicken dish and you're looking at a witbier or Tripel, perhaps, with its citrus-peel and spice high notes. If you're adding lots of garlic, then Weissbier might be even better. A creamy chicken dish will also respond well to a witbier, while fried chicken, with its holy trinity of salt, fat and crisp coating, works brilliantly with something elegant and understated – a Bavarian-style Helles perhaps, where the onus is on honeyed malt rather than hops.

Pizza, Pasta and Bread

What do these items have in common? Wheat and yeast. It therefore stands to reason that wheat-based yeasty beers make excellent partners for these foods, with perhaps the best being the classic Bavarian Helles, which is described as bready for a good reason.

There's a complicating factor, though. Pizza and pasta don't tend to appear naked to the world and generally their bedfellow is tomato-based – a complex mix of sweet, tart and umami flavours that confounds more than a few beer styles (and wines, for that matter). In these instances, I'd go for an amber lager, which is full of bready malt character with some soft caramel notes, which shouldn't offend the tomato. The specialty malts found in amber lager are particularly welcome when it comes to pizza, which has that charred aspect from the oven.

Amber lagers – such as Brooklyn Lager, for example – will also work well with sandwiches, pretty much regardless of the filling. They are delicate and restrained enough to act as an elegant counterpart to all manner of sarnies.

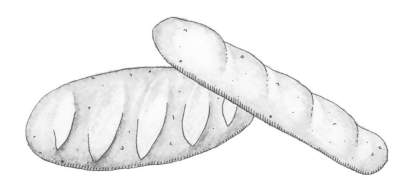

Spices

In Britain, there exists a persistent and unwavering belief that Indian food should be served with pale lager, preferably one with a nod towards some kind of Indian heritage. It's not a bad theory, actually – a crisp pale lager, clean of flavour and full of fizz, refreshes the palate. However, a really good pilsner, with hoppy high notes and plenty of bready malt character is even better.

Beer is the perfect partner to spice. It may be the carbonation, it might be the bitterness, it might be the fact that it's often served chilled, but it is the ideal accompaniment for any number of spicy foods. California-style IPAs, with their citric potency, make a great partner for tacos and burritos – but then, so do witbiers, which have coriander in common and a soothing, almost creamy mouth-feel.

And then there's Weissbier, which is perhaps the best beer of all for spicy food. The yeast spiciness and clove characteristics help, but it's really the big, soft carbonation and the mellow, slightly tart sweetness of the beer that does the trick. It works for Mexican food, spicy Chinese food, Thai food – you name it, it'll do a very a decent job.

Sweet things

Some people are amazed by the suggestion that you might drink beer with desserts, yet chocolate, ice cream and fruit tarts all pair relatively well with beer. One style that really deserves to be highlighted is Imperial Russian Stout, which may sound odd, but bear with me.

IRS can be a very complex beer – sometimes roasty and bitter, other times sweet and rich, very often full of chocolate and espresso character – but whatever the iteration, it usually has something that will work well with sweet food. The chocolatey characteristics make it a natural with, you've guessed it, chocolate dishes, but also ice cream and particularly vanilla and coffee-flavoured desserts such as tiramisu. Other stouts can do similar jobs, but be wary; you need strength here. A low-ABV stout can end up tasting thin and watery when confronted with such rich puddings.

FIVE OF THE BEST: BREWERY PROFILES

Picking just five breweries to represent the world of beer is not easy. I've chosen Cantillon, the most bewitching of breweries, to represent beer's heartland nation, Belgium; Fuller's, to represent London and Great Britain, the birthplace of modern brewing; Pilsner Urquell, the original golden lager and the most famous of the Czech Republic's many great breweries; Sierra Nevada, a Californian brewery that has done more than most to drive America's craft-beer scene and to create the modern obsession with beer; and Stone & Wood, an Australian brewery that demonstrates how good beer has developed and evolved around the world.

Stone & Wood

Once upon a time, Australian brewing concerns used their country's reputation for laidback, humorous, sun-dappled enjoyment to sell beer: this is how millions of Britons ended up drinking Foster's. Things have changed, and now quality is paramount. Antipodean food – from flat whites to avocado on toast – has had a sizeable impact across the world over the past few years. From London to Los Angeles, a laidback but quality-focused approach to food that has its roots in Melbourne and Wellington cafe culture is beginning to blossom, bringing with it all the fruits of the South Pacific.

That now includes beer, although New Zealand was a few steps ahead of Australia in that regard. The likes of Yeastie Boys and Tuatara have led the way, marrying a native preference for cold, clean beer with the diversity of Northern Europe's brewing culture. None of the Kiwi brewers, though, have produced a beer with the breakthrough potential of Stone & Wood's Pacific Ale.

It's a beer that bears the influence of the global scene but in terms of its crucial ingredient, Galaxy hops, it's all Australian. Served fresh, it's full of passionfruit, apricot and melon, and is ridiculously drinkable. 'That flavour … there's nothing like it in any other hop,' says Stone & Wood's director and chief brewer, Brad Rogers. 'When we have punters coming round the brewery, we put a jar of that under their noses. The penny drops: that's where the flavour is coming from.'

Stone & Wood is based in Byron, New South Wales, although most of the beer is now made up the road in their new facility in Murwillumbah. It's a growing company with an eye on where the beer world is going: Stone & Wood recently launched an offshoot brand, Fixation Brewing, to focus on IPAs, which are as popular in Australia as they are elsewhere around the world.

But it's the Pacific Ale that sets Stone & Wood apart. This beer demonstrates that they have taken cues from the American beer revolution but are applying them in a very local way.

Pilsner Urquell

Pilsner Urquell is perhaps the most important brewery of all. The pale lager first brewed in Pilsen in 1842 has conquered the world. Unfortunately, many of its imitators have taken the colour and not much else: the true glory of Pilsner Urquell – especially the unpasteurised version that is increasingly available in Western Europe – is its balance of rich, caramel-inflected malt and spicy Saaz hops.

Like all great brands, Pilsner Urquell's foundation is based on myth. Apparently, the locals grew so sick of the poor quality of locally produced beer that they dumped 36 barrels of it in the town square. City burghers, realising something needed to be done, hired a Bavarian brewer – Josef Groll – and told him to sort things out. The notoriously grumpy Groll produced the first golden lager and the rest is history.

Whether you believe that or not, what is clear is that Pilsen is one of the world's great beer towns, thanks largely to PU (others are produced here, including Gambrinus, which is hugely popular in the Czech Republic but has none of PU's international cachet). Pilsner Urquell is

unavoidable in this quiet, rather old-fashioned Bohemian city of 170,000 people, with many of the historic pubs bedecked in PU branding and the brewery occupying a huge chunk of the city's centre.

As I write, Pilsner Urquell is up for sale, a victim of the global coming together of AB InBev (the world's biggest brewing conglomerate) and SAB Miller, the owner of PU. It's a rare moment of uncertainty for the beer, which has managed to escape the opprobrium experienced by other multinationally owned beers due not only to its quality but also to the fact that it has assiduously courted beer journalists.

Pilsen is well worth a visit. The beer is cheap (At Na Parkánu, a historic city-centre pub that serves unfiltered, unpasteurised PU, it's 42 Czech crowns for half a litre; that's about US$2.00) and a tour of the brewery includes a trip into the underground cellars, which were once used for conditioning the beer in open wooden tanks. It's a damp, atmospheric spot, which somehow manages to make the beer taste even better.

Given that they only produce one beer, it's perhaps no surprise that Pilsner Urquell makes much of the ceremony surrounding its beer. There's an annual 'Master Bartender' competition, which rewards those who are particularly adept at pouring the beer. If this sort of noise is easy to ignore, the beer's significance and continued excellence are not.

Cantillon

Despite being in the heart of a bustling European city, Cantillon's brewery in Brussels can be remarkably tranquil. For a small entrance fee, you can wander around on your own, peering at brewing equipment and the wooden barrels in which the beer develops its unique character. In the attic, where a coolship is used to cool the beer after brewing and, vitally, collect the wild yeast that ferments the beer, you might find yourself completely alone. It's an odd experience: you're in the heart of the de-facto capital of Europe but you feel like you're in a rural brewhouse in the 19th century.

That magic is part of the reason that Cantillon is known and revered around the world, despite the fact that they don't actually produce much beer. Their Lambic beer has become the world's most coveted drop, famous for its dry complexity and vinous bite. Unlike most beers, it has significant acidity (too significant for some), a factor that makes it a wonderful ally to a wide array of rich food.

Current owner Jean Van Roy is the fourth-generation of the Van Roy-Cantillon family; his approach is a little more expansive than that

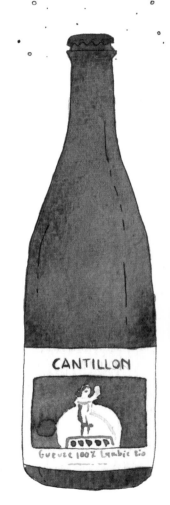

of his forebears (he makes a variety of experimental but delicious beers alongside the classics) but his dedication to the traditions of Lambic brewing is obvious. 'This beer is magic,' he once told me. 'To produce a Lambic, you need time and love. Lambic is totally apart, you can't compare it with other beers. I am a brewer but I am working a bit like a magician.'

Cantillon is not the only Lambic brewer (others of note include Boon and Drie Fonteinen), and there are Belgian blenders, too, who take wort from elsewhere, age it and blend it to produce something unique. But it is Cantillon that has become the standard-bearer for Lambic around the world. There are plenty of brewers who now make wild ale because of Cantillon, and the demand for their beer is perhaps greater than that for any other producer. A brewery that very nearly went out of business in the 1990s as demand in Belgium plummeted looks well set for the future.

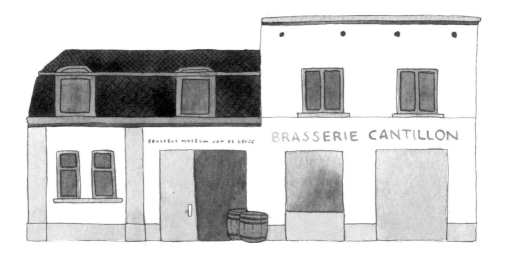

Fuller's

A trip to Fuller's Brewery in Chiswick, West London, is an education. Founded in 1845, the Griffin Brewery, as it's known, is the last remnant of the era when London's great breweries invented modern brewing. During the late 18th and 19th century, the capital of the British Empire was also the capital of world brewing, with huge concerns like Barclay Perkins, Courage and Truman's producing the beer that slaked British thirst.

Fuller's wears this tradition with pride. The beers produced here are classics of the English tradition: Chiswick Bitter, a hoppy session pale ale, London Pride, a moreish, wonderfully dry bitter, and London Porter – perhaps the classic of the style – among the most important. The beer is even brewed using a traditional British method, parti-gyling, whereby a number of beers are made from the same brew.

For all its history, though, Fuller's is not stuck in the past. The brewery has recently invested £2 million in a centrifuge, a piece of kit that removes solids from the beer without the need for harsh and flavour-impacting filtration, which will be used for some of the brewery's bottled, canned and legged products. 'We want to produce the most natural product possible, the most flavour possible,' head brewer, John Keeling, recently told me.

Fuller's may have more history than most but the brewery is also well aware of the modern demand for flavour above all else.

Internationally, Fuller's most famous beer is ESB, or Extra Special Bitter, a 5.5% amber ale that has spawned a style of beer in the USA (but not in Britain; there, ESB just means Fuller's). Flavourwise, it's a balance of Fuller's house marmalade character (which comes from the yeast) and soft toffee and biscuit from the malt. There's also a subdued peppery bitterness. It's a beer worth taking some time over.

Any beer-loving visitor to London should visit the brewery, where an antique brewing kit (which is no longer used) sits alongside some impressively modern equipment. It's the last of London's historic breweries and although the owners say they are committed to remaining on the site, the ludicrous state of London's property market may one day force their hand.

Sierra Nevada

This brewery's pale ale is arguably the most famous product of the craft-beer revolution. It's a clean, hop-forward quaffer, boasting some floral grapefruit character courtesy of the Cascade hops used. Indeed, this is the beer that popularised that most famous of modern American hops: that's how deeply Sierra Nevada's roots go into the story of craft beer.

Sierra Nevada's actual (as opposed to metaphorical) roots are in Chico, Northern California, although there is now another brewery in Mills River, North Carolina. Two breweries? That doesn't sound very craft, although Sierra Nevada's admirable commitment to quality and consistency ensures most are happy to overlook just how big this company has become. Put it this way: Sierra Nevada's beers have not got worse as the brewery has got bigger.

The man behind Sierra Nevada is Ken Grossman. This Southern Californian is not, in all honesty, one of beer's raconteurs; his actions do the talking. Founded in 1979, Sierra Nevada (and a handful of other breweries) emerged into a brewing monoculture, where unthreatening pale lager was pretty much all that was available. Grossman drove himself from Chico to the Yakima Valley to pick up hops and make equipment out of discarded dairy tanks. Ten batches of beer – that is, 10 full brews – were dumped before he was happy with that now-famous Pale Ale.

It hasn't exactly all been upwards from there – American brewing suffered a serious dip in the 1990s – but Sierra Nevada has undoubtedly escaped its humble roots. The solar-powered base in Chico now boasts a 200-barrel brewery, and Grossman himself is a dollar billionaire (according to Bloomberg). Not only its Pale Ale but also the hop-heavy Torpedo and the rich, sweet barley wine Bigfoot are well-known to beer lovers around the globe. And, as American beer has become ever more focused on the hop-heavy, Sierra Nevada has continued to produce a variety (from porter to hefeweiss) that reflects Grossman's own passion for good beer.

GLOSSARY

It is possible to compile a huge and intimidating beer glossary, but it's probably best to stick to the essentials. Here are a handful of terms that are particularly useful.

ABV Short for Alcohol By Volume, it tells you what percentage of the beer is pure alcohol. The higher the number, the stronger the beer.

Adjunct An ingredient used as part of the grain bill that isn't malt. This might be rice, oats, corn, sugar or a number of other largely cereal-based ingredients. Adjuncts are generally used to contribute something desirable to the final beer (such as oats, which adds smoothness to stouts).

Ale One of the two main families of beer. Unlike lager, it is made with top-fermenting yeast and does not traditionally undergo a long period of conditioning.

Brettanomyces Literally 'British Bacteria', this is the wild yeast first identified in British stock ales of the 19th century. It's not considered desirable in most commercial beers but a growing number of brewers are experimenting with it, inspired by the Lambic brewers of Belgium. It can produce a wide range of flavours, from citrus fruit to rustic savouriness.

Boil The point in the brewing process at which hops are added for bitterness and sterilisation takes place.

Cask A container from which unpasteurised, unfiltered beer is served. Traditional in the UK but becoming more common elsewhere, too.

Craft beer A can of worms! Like jazz, it's hard to define but you know it when you taste/hear it. In the most general terms possible, it's beer brewed for flavour rather than the bottom line.

Fermentation The process whereby wort becomes beer, when yeast eats the sugar and creates alcohol and carbon dioxide. More specifically, this is known as ethanol fermentation (ethanol = alcohol).

Hops A green flower traditionally used in beer to add bitterness, flavour and aroma. Different hops have different characteristics: in general, Old-World hops tend to be subtle and spicy while New-World varieties are bold, floral and tropical.

IPA India Pale Ale, a style of beer born in the early 19th century and revived in the late 20th. The modern American version is flamboyantly hoppy, and its popularity has been perhaps the key driver in the rise of craft beer.

Keg A pressurised container used to dispense beer. Most draught beer around the world is served from a keg.

Lager One of the main families of beer (the other is ale), lager has two key characteristics: it is generally bottom-fermenting and spends an extended period of time conditioning (one of lager's meanings in German is 'store'; historically the beer would have been left to condition in cool caves).

Malt Grain that has been partially germinated in order to release its sugar component for brewing. Malt is the most significant solid ingredient of beer.

Mashing The process whereby sugars, flavours and colour are released from the grain at the start of the brewing process.

Wort The sugar-rich liquid that is the result of the brewing process. Fermentation turns it into beer.

Yeast The crucial ingredient that ferments beer. Yeast not only eats sugar and creates alcohol but it also has a decisive say on how a beer tastes.

Published in 2016 by Smith Street Books
Melbourne | Australia
smithstreetbooks.com

ISBN: 978-1-925418-15-6

CIP data is available from the National Library of Australia

Publisher: Paul McNally
Senior editor: Lucy Heaver, Tusk studio
Illustration, design & layout: Daniella Germain

Printed & bound in China by C&C Offset Printing Co., Ltd.

Book 17
10 9 8 7 6 5 4 3 2 1